SINGLE AGAIN

REMARRYING FOR THE RIGHT REASONS

SINGLE AGAIN

REMARRYING FOR THE RIGHT REASONS

Bud & Kathy Pearson

Foreword By Jim Smoke

Regal Books
A Division of GL Publications
Ventura, California, U.S.A.

Rights for publishing this book in other languages are contracted by Gospel Literature International foundation (GLINT). GLINT also provides technical help for the adaptation, translation, and publishing of Bible study resources and books in more than 100 languages worldwide. For further information, contact GLINT, Post Office Box 6688, Ventura, California 93006, U.S.A., or the publisher.

Published by Regal Books
A Division of GL Publications
Ventura, California 93006
Printed in U.S.A.

Library of Congress Cataloging in Publication Data

Pearson, Bud, 1929-
Single again.

Bibliography: p.
1. Remarriage—Religious aspects—Christianity.
I. Pearson, Kathy, 1939- II. Title.
BV838.P4 1985 248.8'4 85-1908
ISBN 0-8307-1032-9

We dedicate this
book to
Lauree, Connie and Mike
who lived
much of it out with us.

Table of Contents

Foreword

Bud and Kathy Pearson have lived through the destruction and debris that divorce has brought into their personal lives. They have individually and together climbed the mountain of new beginnings. They are living in the land beyond divorce and are telling others across America what they have learned and are now learning from their experiences.

Their words of practical wisdom mingled with the gentle nudge of God's Spirit are for all who have known the despair of divorce and have moved on to new life and new hope. For those who are thinking about remarriage, they offer optimism, instruction and guidance based on their own experience and the many whom they have counseled with in seminars and conferences across this country.

Many who are thinking about remarriage or are now living in a remarried state will profit greatly from the real life experiences that are shared in this book. Laugh, live and grow as you travel through these pages and realize anew that God isn't finished with you yet!

—Jim Smoke

Preface

The Bible says God hates divorce, and we've never met a divorced person who disagrees with His opinion. Divorce devastates the people God values so highly, and its effects never end. Nevertheless, we didn't want to write this book. The Christian community frowns upon divorce and remarriage, and few are willing to talk about it. But second marriages are taking place by the thousands, and a huge percentage of them are failing before they get much past the front door. Little has been said or written to help break this cycle of divorce and remarriage.

Our writing, then, has to do with need. We believe that it is far better for the Church to get involved with people who are going to be married again and to help them make a success of it than to have them go from one marriage to another and only know failure. We don't judge remarriage. We believe God's forgiveness is complete, even for divorce. But we're convinced that the only way to break the cycle is to help people understand the principles which make marriages successful.

When we present this material in seminars, we say that it is for those who are fearful of another marriage, those who are hoping to be married again someday, those planning for another marriage, and those already in a second marriage, who, facing the challenges, are crying for help. We don't have all the answers, but there is much here to think about and to apply in any remarriage.

We write out of our experience as students of our own marriage. We decided right away that we were committed to a lifetime of adventuring and growing together. We knew there would be challenges, so we said, "Let's experience both the fun and tears that we know will come. We'll learn and grow together." It has been fun, and there have been many tears, too.

In addition to our own experience, we bring the things we've learned from dozens of remarried couples with whom we have shared life. These people have loved and cared for each other and worked together to build strong marriages. They've had a large measure of success.

We seek to put Jesus Christ at the head of our lives, believing in His love, grace, forgiveness and continuing interest in us. May He be glorified, not because of our successes, but because of His mercy which makes it possible for us, single or remarried, to serve Him.

We have presented this material many times in seminars with single adults and remarried couples. We thank those who have invited us to their churches to share with their people. In doing this, the ideas and concepts were shaped.

Jerry Jones inspired us to think that what we were saying in our seminars was worth putting in book form. He did much to contribute to its formation.

Laurie Clifford put most of the material on paper. She captured our ideas and our hearts and we acknowledge her work with gratitude and heartfelt thanks.

Carol Brown edited the book and worked with us in many meetings to bring the manuscript to its final form.

She was a constant source of encouragement and help.

We also acknowledge the many people who have shared their lives with us along the way. There is no way that we can list the names of all those who have contributed to the writing of this book.

To all of these, and the people of Orange Coast Community Church, who supported us in this endeavor, we say thank you.

1

Kathy's Story

In my mind, I had committed the unpardonable sin. Sitting on the edge of my single bed in a rented house, I knew there was no redemption for me. In agony, I pleaded with the Lord to show me that He loved me. "Lord Jesus, please reach down and touch me," I begged. "Let me know I'm not alone. Why are you so silent? If you've left me, I can't go on."

Exhausted, my emotions spent, I fell silent before God. In the quietness that followed, the Lord put His arms around me. And I began to feel His love bathing my wounds with the freshness of His Holy Spirit. Then He spoke to me. He didn't tell me that the divorce was right. He didn't condone my actions. He simply told me that He loved and forgave me, that His love and forgiveness have no end or final point after which they run out.

As I look back through my life and ponder the events that resulted in the ugliest word I knew—*divorce*—it's difficult to assign *blame*. We are all such a mixture of good and evil in the things we do as well as the things we leave undone. But I can see patterns in my life and being aware of those patterns helps me to understand how the divorce happened.

My earliest memories are happy ones. My mother, a strong, robust woman, put sunshine into my little life on Seattle's rainy days with her smiles and hearty approval of her only daughter. We had a conspiracy against life, she and I, to fight against what was and make it what should be, if only inside ourselves.

"What was" had to do with my father's alcoholism, the disease which ravaged that gentle man who celebrated too often and too well. "What should be" was a Pollyanna homelife we both craved. More than anything, my mother wanted me to be happy.

And I was—because my mother made it all a game. If we had to leave the house because an angry person raged inside it, I knew we would always return in the morning and my father would go to work and my mother would tell me how good his intentions were.

It was a happy, but difficult lesson I learned: that if we close our eyes tightly enough, we can make bad things disappear in the morning. And my mother, the great encourager, sustained me with her love until she died shortly before my first child was born.

She thought I was wonderful. Everything I did was the best. If I sat down at the piano to play Chopsticks, no concert pianist could have pleased her more. If I sang or danced, no artist on stage or screen could have been more talented. She believed in me. And so I believed in myself.

My mother and I practically *lived* in the church. It was a place of refuge for us, a place where right and wrong were clearly defined and right always won. By the time I was 14, I was waiting for Prince Charming, certain he would appear on the horizon at any moment to solidify my American dream.

I found him in church. I fell in love with his father first, and I told myself, *like father, like son.* We'd have a big rambling house full of children, and a white picket fence to protect us from the things that go bump in the night. I promised myself at 14 that this boy and I would make it happen together.

So we became involved. And I became committed—married to him in my heart even before the brief ceremony three years later. *What more do I need for a perfect marriage?* I asked myself, never realizing that common goals and compatible personalities might have something to do with it. *We're both Christians. We don't drink. We don't smoke. We don't mingle with those who do.*

So while I was on tour with my high school choir, I dropped by Boise, Idaho to marry my high school sweetheart, who was now a dashing young Air Force airman. It was a script wonderful enough for the television screen that broadcast all those loving families of the fifties. And I believed it. I knew we would live happily ever after. Why not? We were madly in love.

With our marriage still a secret from everyone but our parents, I returned home to finish high school. Terrified in the walled-up part of me that cradled realities I couldn't allow to spill over and ruin my perfect life, I never let myself think I was anything but deliriously happy over this mysterious event.

Then came the shock of everyday houselife. I graduated from high school and moved, leaving my fan club behind. Where was the intimacy I'd seen on television? Where was the cozy self-contained marriage I'd dreamed about? Because he was in the military, my husband was away half the time, and when he was home, there didn't seem to be much to talk about.

Those were perplexing and depressingly alone days for me. I learned to do all the things housewives did—

cooking and cleaning and managing the budget. Carefully imitating my beloved mother, I made my physical surroundings as perfect as they could be. But about me hung an unexplainable emptiness. I was a grown-up now. I had a husband and a home. But it was all so empty.

And no one talked about the emptiness in those days. This was the late fifties and nice people didn't talk about their problems. As I looked around me, I knew our Air Force town was full of young women who, like me, were struggling to push back depression and meaninglessness each day in the same way they pulled open their drapes and vacuumed their rugs. But we didn't talk about it. The church didn't talk about it. Society didn't talk about it. No one talked about it.

A year and a half later, the traditional solution to a woman's emptiness arrived. My first daughter was born, and I received her with unending joy. While I was expecting Lauree, the greatest tragedy of my life enveloped me. My dear mother, who had been wasting away from cancer, slipped from me into the Father's loving arms. Now I'd been blessed with a daughter, and I vowed to be as marvelous a mother to her as mine had been to me.

Finally, at 19, I was on my way. I had a reason to be—a little daughter who needed me. I had someone I knew I could make a difference for, someone I could fight for and push back the world for, someone I could love with unbounded enthusiasm, someone who would love me back without reservation.

Two more wonderful children sparkled my life in the next 10 years. First Connie, and then Mike. My husband and I were friends. We shared everyday talk about the house and the children. We'd been married when I was 17 and now I was 27. We had a home, three kids, a car in the garage, and a chicken in the pot. We'd accomplished it. We had the American dream. We'd made it come true for us.

Then something happened to unravel my perfect life. Like a flu virus stalking its victim long before it makes its unwelcome presence known, I'd been building a sadness inside, a nothingness, a terrible aloneness. And when the walled-up place inside me could no longer contain what I refused to acknowledge, it trickled over into my everyday houselife, pouring, and then gushing out a torrent of feelings I couldn't explain.

What I remember most is the fear of being alone. Perhaps because I'd never properly grieved over my mother's death, I felt more alone now than when she died. I remember crying without understanding why. I felt more love and compassion from our family doctor than from those closest to me.

The aloneness deepened, growing worse instead of better, and I concluded that God wouldn't be there for me either. *If I'm not to experience His presence, I might as well not go back to church,* I decided. So the Lord sent me a hound of heaven. A woman I knew decided she should go to a particular Bible study and I should go with her because she didn't want to go alone.

I went with her "just once," like a mother walking her child up to the classroom door "but only for the first day of school." And while I was there, the Lord hooked me with an unbreakable line so He could reel me in the next week.

The women in the Bible study talked about radical ideas. They read from a modern translation and I was horrified at their disregard for the King James Bible. They talked about God's unconditional love, the freedom of His Holy Spirit, and about a Christianity that was vital, exciting, and alive.

I had been a working Christian. I had given my life to

Jesus and witnessed and done all the *necessary* things. I loved the Lord and tried my best to do the things the Bible said He wanted. I wanted Jesus to be first in my life. But now, the Lord began to energize my Christianity. He began to put muscles and bones on my faith. And it was the most exciting thing that had ever happened to me.

It began with a stay in the hospital for surgery. And while I was there—by myself for the first time in years—God did surgery on my spirit as well. While I was reading Catherine Marshall's book, *Something More,* God worked a change in me. When I left the hospital, I was free. Everything seemed new and real and precious to me. Most of all, I knew deep down inside that I was precious to my Father.

In the 10 years since my marriage, something awful had happened to me. All the good feelings of my childhood, all the sure-I-can-climb-mountains-just-point-me-in-the-right-direction vigor had seeped from my life. I felt completely inadequate, incapable of anything except caring for my children.

Now my life was turned completely around. I saw myself as a different person, one who was valuable and completely free. I began to feel about myself the way I had felt with my mother, only this time the motivator of my self-worth was the Lord Himself. I was experiencing God's unconditional love which could set me free. It was an exquisitely precious time in my life, but it was very hard on my husband.

While I knew joy inside—joy that bounced deliciously through all the parts of my being—my husband only knew that I was different. And I was becoming more different every day. Although we were both Christians, this was like a conversion experience for me. And with the zeal of a new convert, I determined my husband would share in my excitement.

Just as it was inconceivable to me that we wouldn't marry and live happily ever after, now it was inconceivable to me that our marriage wouldn't enter into the fullness I'd found, that my husband wouldn't discover the Lord the way I had. *Now our marriage will be truly perfect,* I told myself, and I did what I could to make it happen.

Seven years later, our marriage ended in divorce. I had been determined that God would make our marriage perfect, but it didn't happen. In fact, it got worse. We grew even further apart emotionally. And our children were older, asking questions, needing more than simple physical care and affectionate kisses.

Finally, I moved out. I made up my mind that divorce was the only alternative. And when it was over, this was the unpardonable sin for which I could not forgive myself. I'd failed at the very thing I'd prized above all others. The highest goal of my life had vanished forever, and I'd been the one to wield the death blow. I would never be able to forgive myself.

But the Lord forgave me. He came and put His arms around me. He spoke to me with loving and tender words of mercy and grace. He forgave me. And in the years to follow, as I learned to live on my own, He taught me to forgive myself. He showed me how to put the "what could have been's" to rest and get on with the "what can be's."

The Lord Jesus Christ taught me that there's a God on the other side of divorce. And that He's a loving and compassionate God. He showed me that there was redemption and usefulness for my life. He showed me that He binds and heals broken people—whatever the cause of the breaking. And for who He is—for the majesty and greatness of His character—I will praise Him every day of my life.

2

Bud's Story

I was born the year the stock market crashed. Later, people teased me that I was the cause of it. High school sports crowned each year in my small Midwestern town. It was a good place to grow up, a moral place without a vision for the world beyond the county line.

My father was successful in his world. He owned a small but lucrative printing business. In love with the out-of-doors, his goal was to retire with enough money to live as he wished. I believe my mother's strongest desire was peace in her home between her husband and her two sons.

Our home was a practical one. From the time we were very young, our parents trusted us with our lives, certain we would do the right thing. They believed in hard work—lots of it—but what we did with our spare time was up to us.

I remember the joys of boyhood in middle America: the sledding and swimming and knocking around. But those joys were fewer and further apart than I wanted them to be, because I went to work in my father's print shop when I was very young.

After school, I would run home, change my clothes, rush to the shop, and work until a quitting time that depended upon the jobs to be done. Saturdays and summers were the same. Even when I was young, I began striving to be successful and to gain approval in the world I knew.

There's a strange thing about the drive for success. Success can't be found outside yourself. Consequently, I was very insecure. My high school years were difficult ones. I was very sensitive, and I wanted desperately to fit in with the local social scene, but the demands of my already grown-up world made this impossible.

As my awkward teenage years continued, I seemed to be frozen inside myself—a child in a teenage body with the responsibilities of a grown man. I needed to escape. I found that escape with the wrong crowd, and I spent as much time with them as possible.

Upon graduation from high school, my life followed a pre-determined plan. I joined my father full-time in the printing business, began to date the sister of a friend, and married shortly after my nineteenth birthday. When I was 20 years old, my brother and I bought the print shop, and my wife and I had a son.

I had married into a boisterous, affectionate family. My father-in-law always had room on the front porch for one more. It seemed as if the whole neighborhood would congregate there on hot Indiana nights, in a jovial camaraderie that characterizes small towns.

I'd been welcomed by my wife's family even before we were married. Their home was a secure, non-judgmental place. They accepted me. In fact, they thought I was wonderful. And after we married, I gravitated more and more toward the pleasant company of my in-laws.

My wife and I had it all. We had the American dream.

We moved into a house, had plenty of money, and lived in a town where no one thought of locking their doors. We had family and friends around us. Life was good, not just materially, but relationally—as deep as anyone knew relationships could go. And my life would have been fine, if I hadn't hungered for more.

I'd been raised to be a good church-going person. The church we attended was more a social club, propagating a set of rules, than a place for the spiritually hungry to be fed. But for a reason I still don't understand, that hunger was inside of me.

Maybe it came from my mother's conversion experience when I was five or six. The joy in her life at that time had made a tangible impression on me. But she went directly into our liberal church, and was never taught that the Lord wanted to give her more.

Ever since I can remember, I had a funny feeling inside that somehow I'd end up a minister. It was an odd little inkling which was at war with everything my environment had programmed me to be. At 21, I talked with my mother about it.

"I have a call to be a minister," I said. "I don't really understand it because it looks like I'm locked in to this business for the rest of my life. And anyway, I don't know how to become a Christian."

My mother's response was sympathetic, but she didn't know how to help me. Neither did the pastor of our church. When I told him that I wanted to become a Christian, he simply patted me on the back and told me what a good fellow I was. So the Lord sent a missionary to me by way of China.

Erma Pol had been a missionary in Shanghai when the Communists took over. Barely escaping with her life, she found her way to my hometown. She was invited by our young marrieds Sunday School class to be our substitute teacher, and she began to teach the Bible.

An amazing thing happened. Within three months, the class grew from 10 to 80 regular members. No one in our group had ever heard the gospel and we were astounded by the Word of God. It was as if a gourmet meal was set before us every Sunday.

Erma gave us the Word of God for three months before she talked to anyone about becoming a believer. Then she began making the rounds of the class members. She came to our homes sharing the gospel with us and asking us if we wanted to become Christians.

I remember vividly the night she came to our house. When I heard the knock on our door, I knew without being told it was Erma. She shared Christ with us, and that night my wife and I became believers. It was wonderful! The gospel was the most incredible thing I'd ever heard. And I wanted it—eagerly, totally, unconditionally.

My life began again on the evening of December 30, 1953. I told everybody about it. I thought everyone was like I was: hungry to hear but not believing in Christ only because they didn't know how. And in a short time, I saw miracles happen.

My in-laws, my barber and his wife, our milkman and his wife all became Christians. I took a Sunday School class of junior high boys, and in three months we went from three to 30 kids. I gave them all I could, and almost every one of them gave his heart to Jesus.

I was finally on my way. That longing inside had been fulfilled. I knew I had to sell the business, move away and go to school. I was going to be a minister of God's Word, and too much time had been wasted already. So at 25, I sold my share of the business to my brother who was home from the military and ready to settle down. We sold the house as well, and moved to Minneapolis.

I didn't realize until years later what a disastrous effect

this decision had on my marriage. Our security and stability, the foundation of our marriage, had been my wife's family. Now this family was 600 miles away. And without sharing my vision for the ministry, my wife was paying a heavy price.

Years of school, supporting myself all the while, and church work followed. In the next 21 years, I pioneered four new churches. My zeal for the Lord's work was unbounded. I couldn't seem to give enough of myself to the cause of spreading the gospel. My faith was expressed in my works, and I worked at "the Lord's work" day and night.

But our marriage—which had been based on the security of small town relationships and ways of life—floundered. My wife directed her frustration with our life at herself. She had no one to help her understand that she was locked into a life she hadn't chosen.

Those were the days before counseling—before the church or the world reached out to help ordinary people understand themselves. Psychiatry and counseling were for "mental cases." And we weren't crazy, we were just terribly needy of insight, communication and understanding.

As the years progressed, there was occasional sunshine in our marriage, and from time to time breaks in the clouds helped us go on. In the late sixties, small groups began to appear in the church, groups in which it was acceptable to open up and share honestly. And every now and then we encountered a bit of information here, a person or situation there, that seemed to make a difference.

Toward the end of our marriage, counseling was no longer a foreign word in the world of "normal" people, and we were seeing a psychologist, every week. After several sessions, he asked me, "What have you got against divorce?" It was his opinion that our marriage would never be a whole one, that the differences between us were too great. He said that it was a hopeless relationship with too much anguished time as history.

"I don't think you'll be able to change enough to make it work," he said. I told him that since divorce wasn't a possibility for us, it would never happen. And during the time we continued with counseling, our life together did begin to improve. It was the best time we had had in our relationship, and it seemed as if we were finally on our way.

Apparently, that time wasn't long enough. We weren't strong enough to withstand outside stresses. Life tore at us, and our newfound strength crumbled. After 26 years of marriage, I found myself at the Mayo Clinic, with an illness no one could diagnose.

At my last conference there, the doctors said, "There's nothing physically wrong with you. You have an enormous conflict in your life. Your pain is real, but it doesn't have a physical origin. And until you resolve this conflict, whatever it is, you won't be well."

So I made the decision not to continue in my marriage. The divorce was the most devastating experience in my life. I resigned from my church, not wanting to put the congregation through the inevitable turmoil of a divorced pastor, and moved to Southern California without much sense of why, only knowing that I had to be somewhere.

My life was gone. Everything I'd built, everything I'd worked for was over. There was no place in the church for a divorced pastor, but I didn't want to be anywhere else. I considered returning to the printing business, but I couldn't reconcile that with what I knew to be God's call on my life. So I took menial jobs, and waited for the Lord to open doors for me.

I remember sitting on the floor of my rented apartment, staring at the walls, and wondering, *What has happened to me?* All my life I had been "successful" in everything I'd done. And now I was completely alone in an unfurnished apartment, in a city I didn't even like, stripped of everything that had meaning for me.

I had failed everyone who cared about me. I had sinned against God. I knew I was a failure. And I didn't know where to turn. So I decided to sit down with my Bible, to spend time reading it, and to try to get to know God better. During this process, a little phrase from Paul's experience on the tempestuous sea caught my attention. He stood up in the boat and said, "So keep up your courage, men, for *I have faith in God* that it will happen just as he told me." Acts 27:25 (italics added).

The phrase that caught hold of me was "I have faith in God that it will happen just as he told me." *I have faith in God. I have faith in God. I have faith in God.* I began to tell myself this over and over again. *I have faith in God. I believe that His promises are true. Therefore, He has a future for me. His way is the way out of the hell I'm experiencing.* Over and over, day after day, week after week, month after month, I had faith in God. I believed He had a wonderful future for me.

Slowly, painfully, the Lord began to rebuild my life, to give me a place in His ministry again. As I trusted Him, giving Him the only thing I had left to offer, He took my trust and turned it into a glory and a praise to His name. And I found that my usefulness to Him wasn't over. I found He hadn't written me off. He forgave me, renewed me, and put me back on my feet.

I have learned that, just as God says in Romans 8:38-39, there is nothing that can separate me from His love and provision—not even divorce. I have learned that God's forgiveness is complete. He really does separate us from our sins just as far as the East is from the West. The scars remain and the pain lingers, but His faithfulness is forever.[1]

3

Grow, Grow, Grow!

We were on staff at Garden Grove Community Church when we first began to hold seminars on remarriage. Shortly before our marriage, Jim Smoke asked us to speak at a national singles' conference. "Just do a workshop," he said. "Tell about what led up to your remarriage and share some of the things you've learned."

The conference came only three weeks after we were married. By this time, we were barely speaking to each other. We had returned from a glorious honeymoon to the jarring realities of a second marriage, and now we were committed to speak about remarriage before hundreds of people.

Somehow, we lived through the workshop. Apparently, we did an adequate job because we were invited to do it again. As we began to experience healing in our own lives, we saw the need for an honest discussion of remarriage, and developed it into an all day seminar.

Why Talk About Marriage to Single Adults?

Why talk about marriage to single adults? Especially

to those who have been married before? There's a misconception that love is lovelier the second time around. *After all,* you think as you approach marriage, *I've learned so much about marriage already. This time I'll do it right.*

The facts, however, say something different. Today in America, for every married couple, there is a single adult. Within three years, a great percentage of these people will be married. If it's a first marriage, 40 to 50 percent will end in divorce. If it's a second marriage, statistics indicate that 60 to 70 percent will end in divorce. If it's a third marriage, the numbers go almost off the charts.

What goes wrong when people remarry? Everything that went wrong the first time, and more. The basic reason so many marriages fail is that people marry for the wrong reasons. They haven't grown as individuals. They think marriage will solve their problems, but marriage isn't meant to be the solution to personal insecurities.

Often, when couples remarry, they simply shift all their hang-ups—compounded by the pain, bitterness, and trauma of divorce or bereavement—to the new marriage. It's not surprising that the marriage isn't what it should be. It's not surprising when it fails.

We believe this trend can be reversed. We believe marriage can be a happy place where two people are free to be everything God wants them to be. So we believe it's important to talk about remarriage. The principles that will make a second or third marriage work are the same ones that will strengthen a first marriage. And the sooner we begin talking about the ingredients of a good marriage, the better.

We were invited to share at a church in Newport Beach, California. When we walked in, we found quite a few singles in their early twenties among the audience of 125 people. We thought, *What will these young people gain from our seminar?* We had spoken before to never married, widowed, or divorced singles, but never to young people who were just starting out in life.

We presented our material, hoping it would touch them in some way, and after it was over, they came up to us as a group. In different ways, each one said the same thing. The principles we taught applied to their lives. Krista said, "I'm a teacher. Now I can understand why my kids at school act the way they do after their parents have separated."

Few of us remain untouched by divorce. If we haven't been scarred by it personally, it has devastated someone we know or someone the Lord will bring to us in the future. The principles involved in preparing for a happy life—single or married—are universal. They are for everyone to consider.

We believe in marriage. We believe God created marriage for our benefit. But we don't believe marriage makes anyone a whole person. You are a person of God's creation just as you are. He means for you to be whole, whether you're single or married and in marriage, two halves don't make a whole. Our friend, Dr. Robert Merkle, says, "Marriage isn't a bicycle built for two. It's two good bicycles going in the same direction."

God wants marriage to be a beautiful experience. He didn't create it as a test of endurance. Marriage can and should be a positive, growing statement of life. Every principle we share in this book comes from personal experience—if not our own, then from those we've counseled. We believe that everything in this book is practical, basic, and universal.

The Classroom of Your Life

Shortly after we were married, everything fell apart. It became an explosive situation after only one week. We decided right then that we would solve the problem by sitting in the school room of our own marriage. We agreed to see our lives as a classroom. We decided to observe what was going on, talk about it, and to grow. This is something everyone can do. Single or married, you can use your life as a classroom, with the idea of turning every experience into a plus.

God wants to change our negatives into positives. The harder you fight against change, the more you battle against life and struggle to hold back the things that will make you grow, the more miserable you will become. Only when you begin to relax and enjoy life as God brings it to you, will you find yourself becoming a positive, growing, and interesting person.

All positive change in our lives comes through growth. And we don't grow overnight. Growth is a process. The goal of our lives should be to *grow*. The questions of our lives should be: Am I growing? Am I maturing? Am I becoming more like Jesus? If we set out on a pattern of growth, change will follow naturally.

Accepting Yourself Where You Are

The foundation of growth is to begin to see yourself as God sees you. You are a precious person to Him. Do you know why? The answer is simple. Because He made you.[1]

Think about it for a moment. Close your eyes and concentrate on the Creator, the maker of everything that is. Now ask yourself, "Would He make something inferior? And when it came time to create the beings made in His image, would He make one that wasn't valuable to Him?"

The fact is, that God made you because He wanted someone just like you. He wants you for all eternity. You're so special to Him that even if you had been the only person who ever lived, He still would have sent His Son to die just for you.

When you see yourself as the priceless person that you are, you can begin to grow. You can begin to become everything God meant you to be. As you praise Him and allow Him to work in your life, He'll use everything—even the negative things—to form and shape you.

Enter the Joy of Growing—as an Individual

You are a person in your own right, and you can enter the joy of growing. You're not an extension of your parents. You're not an extension of your boyfriend or girlfriend. You're not an extension of your former mate. You're not an extension of your children. You are an individual, and your individuality is your birthright.

Tell yourself, "I'm special. I'm unique. I have qualities that make me one of a kind. I don't need to hear this from someone else to believe it. It's God's opinion of me, so I believe it. I don't need another person to validate my existence."

We get ourselves into trouble when we look to other people to fulfill our needs. We search for that one person and make him or her the center of our emotional universe. Suddenly, that person becomes responsible for our well-being. And when he or she fails, we're on an emotional landslide.

It's unrealistic to think that anyone else can fulfill all or even most of your needs. And while marriage does satisfy many of our needs, the purpose of marriage is to love and encourage each other, and to build a life together which expresses unity to a fractured world.

When you have a relationship with the Lord Jesus Christ, He has promised to fill you up with His Holy Spirit.[2] This means you can be open and growing, willing to risk His love for you, willing to let *Him* satisfy your needs.

A Diamond in the Rough: Life Is a Process

Some of us are completely taken aback when we go through a negative experience. We're knocked off our feet because we don't know how to handle it. You aren't alone if this is the way you tend to respond. It's the human condition because sin has brought distance between us and our Father.[3]

When these negative experiences happen, think of yourself as a diamond. When diamonds are mined, they're unrecognizable to anyone but an expert. They're rough and rugged and dirty. But as the stones are cut and polished, they become recognizable. They begin to shine and people see them and say, "Oh, isn't it beautiful."

We're like freshly mined diamonds in the expert's hand. God taps here and chips there—and it hurts—but the dirt falls away and the rough edges become smooth. Then the brilliance of His creation begins to shine through, and others say, "What a beautiful person that one is."

Take heart because you have an opportunity to grow. You have the chance to see your life from a new point of view—from God's perspective. You can reach a place in your life where you've never been before. You can believe God's opinion of you. You can accept yourself with all your history (just the way He accepts you) and you can believe that your life is being molded by God Himself. He loves you and wants you to have a full, rich life right now.

It's possible to keep growing spiritually for all of your life. Establish this as a goal. Say to yourself, "I'm going to grow spiritually for the rest of my life. I'll never let a time come when I think I've arrived."

The greatest way to achieve this is to become acquainted with the Word of God. Because it's a dynamic force, unique among all writings, the more time you spend in it, the deeper and richer it becomes. And as you grow in your understanding of who God is, you grow in your understanding of what life is about. The more we know about God, the more we know about ourselves because we are made in His image.

You also have the capacity to grow emotionally and intellectually for all of your life. Beyond growing spiritually, make it a life goal to exercise your intellect and stretch your emotions. The more you use your mind, the fuller your life will be, right now as well as in old age.

You *can* probe, be curious, read, study, converse and expose yourself to things that will stimulate your mind. All these will enhance the possibilities for you to have a beautiful life. Tell yourself, "I want to grow as a person," and put yourself in that position.

Two Halves Don't Make a Whole

At the heart of learning to love and accept yourself is getting to know yourself. This may sound strange because after all, who should know you better than yourself. But in this fast-paced world, we're constantly on the run. And we're constantly searching for something or someone to fill the void inside.

Because of this basic lack of self-worth, we don't consider ourselves worthy of our own time and attention. We don't take the time to be quiet with ourselves, to ask ourselves about our goals and desires for the future. If we don't value ourselves, why should we value our own opinions? Why should we plan for the future? Why should we respect our own likes and dislikes?

It's your life and you only get to live it once. So take time to know yourself. Take time to like yourself. Take time to plan for what your life will be. So much of it—especially who your partner will be—is under your control.

Exercising Your Greatest Power

One of the most blessed aspects of life is your power to choose, and it's absurd not to exercise your options. If you take time to think about it, it's unthinkable to throw your life up for grabs.

A fundamental principle of Christianity is that we should love others *as we love ourselves.*[4] This presumes that we do indeed love ourselves, that we value and respect ourselves. Then just as we learn to set ourselves free from living by others' expectations, we can set others free from living by ours.

Just as you've been set free, you set others free to be everything God wants them to be. But to find this freedom you need to see yourself as a whole person now. God sees you as a whole person. Begin to adopt His point of view.

Several years ago, we had the opportunity to go to Japan, the Philippine Islands, and Hawaii under the auspices of the Air Force. We knew when we left Los Angeles that we'd be busy from 12 to 14 hours a day for the entire three weeks. And we knew there would be some rough times during those three weeks.

They had us *scheduled.* And when we looked at the schedule, we felt like folding up and staying home. It was frightening to consider because it was a new experience for us. We weren't seasoned world travelers and speakers. We knew we'd be flying in Air Force planes, traveling to remote areas, and meeting new people day and night.

Finally, we talked it over, prayed about it, and said, "OK, here's what we're going to do. No matter what were doing, no matter how stressful it gets, no matter how unpleasant the circumstances seem, we're going to determine right now by God's grace that we'll enjoy every minute of it, no matter what."

We had already adopted this as a philosophy of life, but we restated it to each other. When we returned from that trip, we found we had enjoyed everything we'd done. It had been a chance to expand our horizons, to touch other people's lives, to do things we'd never done before and might never do again. At times, it was just as stressful as we imagined it would be, but because we'd decided to grow with it rather than to resist it, it was just as wonderful as we knew it could be.

Single life has many stresses, but it is replete with opportunity for growth and vitality. You can grow right where you are. Begin with your job. Tell yourself, "My job is important and meaningful." Tell yourself the same thing about the other everyday activities common to us all.

All experiences in life can be dynamic, if you let them be. Allow the Lord Himself to give you a zest for life. This growing attitude will add sparkle to your life, adding enjoyment and blessing to everything you do and allowing you fulfillment and meaning in your life whether you remain single or someday marry.

4

The 50-50 Proposition

A woman came up to us after our seminar at a singles' conference. Patricia was in her thirties, a vital woman with an obvious zest for life. "This has been one of the best days of my life," she said, "because today, for the first time in my life, I really understand that I am where I am because I made the decisions that put me here."

You can't take responsibility for where you're going until you assume responsibility for your past. When you do that, you can take charge of your future. Knowing your humanity, knowing that all your choices won't be perfect or even right, you can trust God to use *everything* for your ultimate good in the process of life, and to make you all He intended from the beginning.

What seemed negative to you at one time may in fact be very positive, a necessary ingredient in the long run. Consider the stained glass windows that adorn churches around the world. Nothing is more beautiful than these windows as the rays of the sun stream through them. But these windows are made of broken glass, chiseled and fitted under the artist's hand. Likewise, God mends broken people and makes us into what He wants us to be.

Accepting Responsibility for Your Choices

In our culture, we're taught to blame other people for our problems. It's almost a tradition. We blame the government. We blame the media. We blame the environment. We blame our employers and our parents, our children and our friends. We even blame our ex-mates.

Life is a process of decisions—a lot of little ones, and a few big ones along the way. Even not deciding is a decision. Often it's not the big decisions that cause problems, it's all the little ones leading up to them.

The decision to marry is a big decision. But it's the culmination of many small ones. And after you've married, it's the ordinary everyday choices that determine its success. We've already said that the greatest power you have is your power to choose. But before you can make good choices for your future, you must accept the ones you've made in the past. Whatever your past has been, in Christ, it's forgiven. The Lord has promised to recycle the negatives. Let Him do it.[1]

How much time do you spend bemoaning the fact you weren't born into royalty? It's a fantasy for some people, but it's our guess you don't spend much time longing for it to be true. It would be a waste of time, wouldn't it?

It makes just as much sense for you to spend useless energy playing the "what if" game with your past. What if my parents had been different? What if my home had been different? What if my spouse had been different? The past is gone, and all the "what if" game does is rob you of your future.

In our counseling ministry we meet two kinds of people—those who take too much responsibility for where they are in life, and those who don't take enough.

People who accept 50 percent seem to be in the minority, yet we believe we must do just that in any relationship. You are only partially responsible for its successes and only partially responsible for its failures.

Imagine that you've encountered a warm, witty, and wise financial counselor. You put your faith in his guidance and allow him to invest all your money. For those of us who don't have any money, let's say it's $50,000. A year later, you find out this man has made some unwise decisions and all your money is gone.

How can you be 50 percent responsible for what happened to your money? You only made one decision—the decision to let him invest your money. He made hundreds of decisions over the course of the year. But the 50-50 principle says that whatever your part in the matter was—small or great—your part equals 50 percent. You made the decision to put the money into his hands, and that's your 50 percent. Not 50 percent of the blame, but 50 percent of the *responsibility.*

How Much Is Enough?

For those who accept too little responsibility, the 50-50 principle restores a sense of power to their past. Because we feel helpless, we cling blindly to the weapon of blame. "It's his fault." "It's her fault." "Look at what they did to me." We feel that we're victims, and so we use the only weapons we have: bitterness, hatred, and negative thoughts.

It gives us something to do, something to hang on to. We have a feeling of power as we direct our negative emotions toward the person or situation that hurts us. But what we don't see is that we're beating empty air. We're clubbing *nothing* to death. The past is gone and if we don't let it go, we'll only carry the hurting over into our future.

For those of us who accept too much responsibility, the 50-50 principle relieves us of the need to drown in guilt. When we realize that the other person is responsible for his share—his 50 percent—of what went wrong, the self-imposed false burden of having ruined someone else's life is lifted from us.

There are exceptions to the 50-50 principle, just as there are exceptions to most things in life. But it is true in almost every case. Kathy's mother was married for many years to her dad who was an alcoholic. Although they stayed together until her mother's death, it was a difficult marriage because of his drinking.

To everyone around—the neighbors, friends, and even family—it seemed that her husband was completely responsible for the troubled marriage. One day Kathy asked her mother, "Didn't you know he drank before you married him?"

"Yes," she answered.

"Then why did you marry him?" Kathy asked.

"Because I thought I could change him."

That was her 50 percent!

The decision to marry carries with it the possibility of divorce. Whether or not you believe in divorce, it is a possibility. So from the beginning, there's the responsibility to create a marriage that will be a success. But no one can do it alone. Because marriage is a partnership, it takes two *equally responsible* partners to make it work.

If your previous marriage ended in divorce, no matter what the circumstances, you must search through your past relationship and understand what made up your 50 percent. You must accept that you were neither the only victim nor the only culprit.

Did you take your spouse for granted? Did you have bad attitudes which may have caused your spouse to become disillusioned? Did you put all your emphasis on the children? Did you work too much, not leaving time for play? Did you smother your spouse?

Were you willing to share your feelings? Did you actively encourage your spouse to become everything the Lord intended? These are only a few questions to review as you search for your 50 percent. But remember, you are searching for *responsibility,* not *blame.*

If you feel that you behaved perfectly in your marriage, then look back at your behavior before you were married.

Were you involved sexually? Did you take time to know yourself and your future spouse? DId you marry impulsively? Did you say, "Well, I don't like certain things about my fiance, but those will change after we're married"?

Manipulation and the Real Meaning of Submission

Manipulation is devastating to a relationship. And manipulation is so clever. It usually comes in a beautiful package, disguised in good intentions and generous feelings. "His life would be so much better if he'd just change this." "She would be so much happier if she wouldn't do that." "Well, I'll just help this person change."

Manipulation goes hand in hand with unrealistic expectations. We believe marriage should be a certain way, and when it fails to conform to our preconceptions, we begin to manipulate, to help it fit what we think it should be. Often our manipulation is so subtle, we aren't even aware of it. That's what makes it so dangerous. From our point of view what we're trying to accomplish is so logical, so *necessary,* anyone would understand.

In Ephesians 5:21, Paul tells married couples to adapt themselves to each other, not to adapt each other to themselves. This is the meaning of submission—adapt yourself, make room for who the other person is, accommodate your mate. This is the character of a true Christian marriage.

We spoke with Roger, a young man who surprised us by his wisdom. "I've been dating a wonderful girl," he said. "Linda is beautiful, intelligent, and kind, but one day I went to her apartment. I couldn't believe it! Her place was so neat, a dustball would have seemed like a major catastrophe.

"Now, I'm the kind of guy who likes to bring the garage indoors. I just don't think I could live in a tidy world like hers. So I guess I'll have to break off our relationship and look for someone else."

When we talked to Roger later, he said he'd found another girlfriend. "Her place is a mess," he said with a grin. "In fact, I'd like it to be a little more organized. But I'm sure I can adapt myself to a Mrs. Mess a whole lot better than I could to a Mrs. Clean."

Roger was smart. Rather than marry with the hope he could change her, which brings manipulation, he chose to accept the reality of the way things were.

Another reason for the 50-50 principle is that in your heart you know it to be true. On the surface, you might feel "I'm all wrong," but inside there's a nagging suspicion that you haven't been treated as you'd like to be. On the surface, you might feel, "He's all wrong," or "She's all wrong," but inside there's a festering guilt because you know you've been wrong too.

The fear of failure is the flip side to the fear of being failed. Both are terrifying. Both say, "I can't admit I let you down." Or "I can't admit you let me down." Either is incredibly difficult to accept. But when you admit the human condition—that you fail others and they fail you—you're moving toward forgiveness, the wonderful word that says, "It's OK. It's over. We can tear this page out of the book of records."

Recognizing Our Human-ness: Pride, Anger and Forgiveness

A clear understanding of the human condition is essential to the process of taking 50 percent of the responsibility. Until we understand we're sinners—that we miss the mark—we will continue to try to justify our particular point of view. Only when we acknowledge our sinfulness can we move to God's point of view. Only then can we understand His grace.

An insidious attitude called pride is at the heart of our inability to admit our sinfulness. It lurks in the most unlikely places. It colors the I'm-always-right people, the I'm-always-wrong people, and the in-between people. Pride holds on to our own opinions rather than giving in to God's opinions.

The Old Testament tells us about King Saul. He knew the kind of man God wanted him to be, but he was fearful of losing his prestige, of weakening *his* hold on the kingdom. Pride, fear, and anxiety characterized his response to God. If Saul had accepted that he was king simply because God made him king, he would have ruled long and prosperously. He would have been free to enjoy what God had given him.

Instead, Saul believed he was king because of his own merit. This meant he had to protect his position, justify his actions, and hunt down all threats to eliminate them. Because of this, Saul was insecure and miserable, constantly plotting to kill David even though David had proved he wouldn't harm him.[2]

Jesus said, "You will know the truth, and the truth will set you free."[3] When you set aside your pride and accept God's opinion of you—that you're a sinner, but that His love and acceptance aren't based on your performance—you will be free. You will know His forgiveness and begin to function in a completely new way.

The anxieties and fears of not being able to measure up are gone. You no longer have an image to protect. You can say, "I was responsible." and it doesn't catch in your throat. Instead, it becomes a release, the pathway to new freedom that enables you to soar.

Accepting responsibility means not rationalizing your past. It's easy to say, "Well, yes, I had a bad temper, but it was because of all the negative things he did." Or, "Well, yes, I was always gone, but it was because she nagged at me constantly." This sort of rationalization makes the other person the bad guy, and only gets you off the hook temporarily.

Accepting responsibility also means recognizing, accepting and then letting go of your anger. Psalm 4:4 says, "In your anger do not sin." In other words, be angry, get over it, and get going again.

When you give in to the anger, nurturing it with your thoughts and actions, you create an attitude of bitterness and hostility. If you've been divorced for a year or two and still have bitterness toward your ex-spouse, you are still emotionally chained to that relationship.

Mary, a young woman in her twenties, came to our office. Frequently stopping for tears, she poured out her story in anger and frustration, blaming her ex-spouse for everything that had gone wrong in the marriage. He hadn't been a good provider, a good father, a good lover, a good anything. He was just no good. And she was glad to get rid of him.

That's what Mary was saying, but the bitterness in her eyes told us she'd never be "rid of him" unless she changed her attitude. We began to pray with her, counseling her over the weeks and gently asking her to consider what had really happened in her marriage.

As she began to accept her share of the responsibility for the failure of the marriage, she began to let go of her bitterness and resentment. She began to understand why her ex-husband behaved the way he did. She began to tell herself that he had done the best he could, given who he was. She began to wish him well and pray that God would bless him.

Mary's life began to change. Because her thoughts were different, her feelings were different, and soon her actions changed as well. Now she's on the grow spiritually. She's in control of her future because she has accepted her 50 percent of the responsibility for what happened in the breakup of her marriage.

The Lord Jesus Christ wants this freedom for all of us. He has promised to break the chains that bind us. We just need to cooperate with Him and to believe His truth. This is the truth which, as it's worked out in our lives, will surely set us free. Living life successfully as a single adult requires this freedom. Growing is dependent on leaving the hurt and pain, the anger and bitterness in the past. Wholeness of attitude makes for an exciting life. And, should God bring you a person to marry, you will be read.

5
Leaving Your Past in the Past

We are aware of only seven things in life. Three of these have to do with time—past, present, and future; the other four things are God, ourselves, others, and the world around us. That's the sum of our awareness.

The first area of awareness—our past—often colors the rest, serving as a sort of parole officer. This is because most of us are coming from two very negative experiences: guilt and failure, and are haunted by the feeling that the past wasn't good enough.

Strangely enough, we feed these feelings of guilt and failure by transferring them into the future. And while the future may not be exactly like the past, it becomes parallel. We project our feelings about the past into the future, and the two inevitably begin to look alike.

Our vision of the future becomes colored by two things: anxiety and fear. Subconsciously, our mental tape goes something like this: "I failed before (guilt) therefore I'll probably fail again (anxiety)." If we play this tape often enough, we become afraid to launch out and really live. So we become prisoners of the past in self-fulfilling prophecies.

On a human level, we try to deal with this predicament by saying, "I'll reform my past." It's an impossible task, but since it's a subconscious process, we don't think it through logically. We simply tell ourselves, "I'll turn over a new leaf. I'll be different."

As we work toward a future that will be better than the past, establishing goals and setting standards, we often catch ourselves thinking, "I'll do this and this. Then when I've done it, I'll feel good about myself and I won't have to deal with guilt and failure any more."

When we think like this, we are letting our past rule our present which determines our future, and we're rendered useless in the present. The present becomes merely a passage to the future. We don't take time to feel good about ourselves now because we haven't yet atoned for the past. But we keep thinking that the time will come. Any day now, we'll have reformed the past, formed the future, and be able to enjoy the present. Unfortunately, this blissful time never comes because we continually fall short of our own standards, mess up our goals, and have to start the process from the beginning.

Accepting God's Forgiveness and Cleansing

The only solution to this predicament is the one given by God Himself. How does He tell us to deal with the failures of our past? Through forgiveness. Romans 8:28 says, "And we know that in all things God works for the good of those who love him, who have been called according to his purpose."

We could paraphrase this verse like this: "I know you're going to make some dumb decisions because you're a human being. I know you're going to blow it, and mess up in a lot of what you try to do. And you're going to feel guilty. You're going to feel like a failure. But that's where I take over. That's what I'm here for. I'm here to flood your whole being with forgiveness, and to set you free so you can let go of the past, live in the present, and built a beautiful future."

We can't reform the past, but God forgives the past when we come to Him through Christ. We memorize John 3:16 in Sunday School. "For God so loved the world that he gave his one and only Son, that whoever believes in him shall not perish but have eternal life." But not many of us know the next verse. "For God did not send his Son into the world to condemn the world, but to save the world through him." God doesn't condemn us. We condemn ourselves with feelings of guilt and failure. God allows us to have those feelings in order to draw us back to Himself. But we sentence ourselves with them. God doesn't want to sentence you. He wants to forgive you and to set you free through His Son Jesus Christ.

Sometimes, we get the idea that the Bible is a whip to bring us into line. But it's not. It's a love letter full of mercy and grace. Most of us feel we have to whip ourselves for a while. We have to grovel and kick ourselves until we feel *really bad* about what we've done. Then maybe we can come to God and be forgiven. We don't understand that the greatest sin of all is turning from our Lord. And the whole time we're groveling, and lecturing ourselves and promising never to do it again, our backs remain turned to God.

God forgives you immediately when you trust Christ. This is the essence of the Christian life. Accept this great reality, and you can live fully.

When God forgives you, He also forgets what you've done wrong. When we say God forgets our sins, we mean He *acts as if they never happened.* And that's what He wants you to do. He wants you to live in the present, completely freed from your past. Your past failures are as if they never even happened when you receive forgiveness in Christ.[1] This is God's desire for us. He wants us to experience the joys of life, completely free from any negative hold of the past.

Even though divorce involves sin, it is not the unpardonable sin. God's Word says Christ died for all your sins—big and little, simple and complicated. And it speaks of only one unpardonable sin—the blasphemy of the Holy Spirit, the continual rejection of His attempts to draw someone to God.[2] Divorce is *not* an unpardonable sin, and God forgives us completely when we trust Christ.

There's only one kind of person who doesn't experience God's forgiveness—the one who won't admit he needs it and doesn't accept this free gift. Jesus expressed it perfectly when He spoke to the woman at the well. This woman was a Samaritan and was looked down upon by everyone in her society.

Jesus told her, "Whoever drinks the water I give him will never thirst. Indeed, the water I give him will become in him a spring of water welling up to eternal life."[3] Jesus pointed out to the woman that she had had five husbands, and she was living with another man at the time. But when He offered her living water, she believed Jesus, and she became His messenger to Samaria.

Jesus never condemned her. He simply forgave her and offered her a new life. Condemnation comes from Satan. His purpose is to destroy your usefulness to God, make you miserable, cause you to crouch in the shadows of your past and render you unable to serve God in the present.

In our need to atone for our past, we ruin our present. This affects us at all levels of life. God wants us to accept His forgiveness. When we realize that God wants to forgive us, we can be full of hope. We begin to sense that life will be good, that we can live fully in the present, and that we have a great future ahead of us.

Loving God

There are certain principles built into God's creation, and this principle of hope is one of them. Each day is divided into darkness and light. When morning comes, it's as if God is saying, "Come alive again! See. I've given you a new day. Your past is gone. You have a new beginning!"

If we're truly living in a forgiven present, the grudges of the past begin to disappear. We're so busy enjoying the present, there just isn't any energy left to nurture hatred from the past. It's true that some things have been very damaging, but God has promised to recycle them.

Forgiveness is the key to freedom in all seven areas of awareness. When we deal with the past through forgiveness, accept His freedom for the present, and look forward to a forgiven future, something wonderful happens to the other four areas of awareness. How does it affect the way you feel about God, yourself, others, and the world around you?

It makes you feel wonderful about God. You know He's not out to get you or to condemn you; He's out to love you. Now you can have a beautiful relationship with Him. You know He isn't asking you to be perfect, but to live in His perfect forgiveness.

This is what the Ten Commandments are about. They set an impossible standard—one which no one can attain. God knew this even when He gave the commandments to Moses. He didn't discover through trial and error that His commandments, His standards of righteousness, were impossible for human beings. He knew it from the beginning.

Each one of us has broken His commandments. You

may think, *I've never committed murder.* But Jesus said if you've ever hated someone, you've broken this commandment. Or you may think, *I've never committed adultery.* But Jesus said if you've ever looked at someone with lust, you're guilty.

Who has ever kept the greatest commandment perfectly? "Love the Lord your God with all your heart and with all your soul and with all your mind and with all your strength."[4] Not one of us. God wants us to know we can't keep His standards perfectly. This isn't so we'll feel guilty and worthless. It's so we'll come to Him, accept His forgiveness and depend on His righteousness, not our own.

Forgiving Ourselves and Forgiving Others

Now that you feel good about God, how do you feel about yourself? You can feel marvelous when you truly accept and understand what God has done for you. But, because of our human nature, we sometimes lose sight of this truth. The devil and the world and our own pride draw us away, and we have to return to God's Word, again and again. But it's always there, giving us that exhilarating sense of forgiveness and the wholeness it brings through Jesus Christ.

How do you respond to others and to the world around you in this chain of awareness? There's a psychological principle that says the way you feel about yourself is what you'll express to others. When you can say, "I'm a wonderful person. I'm a forgiven person. God loves me," then your responses to others and to the world will be in line with this self-image.

When people are always critical of others, you can be sure it reveals something of the way they feel about themselves. When people feel loved and forgiven, they treat others in the same manner.

When Kathy was going through her divorce, she

found herself going next door to spend time with a neighbor who listened without asking a lot of questions. She just listened and accepted. Because of her neighbor's love, Kathy was able to get in touch with God's love. We are God's hands and ears and smiles on this earth. And we have the ability to lead others to His love.

If God seems far away and untouchable to you, look for Him in His people. Find a loving church. Get involved in a small group of caring people. Choose friends who have loving attitudes. Associate with positive Christians who love and accept you.

Janet counsels with us simply because she needs to talk about her feelings. She has a boyfriend, an ex-husband with whom she's friendly, and girlfriends, but she doesn't share her deepest self with any of them. Wisely, she realized her need for total acceptance and came to a counseling situation when she couldn't find it elsewhere.

As you understand God's love, you can believe in His forgiveness and extend it to others. God says, "Don't judge. Leave that up to me."[5] That's what forgiveness is. It's suspending your judgment of yourself and of other people.

Be patient with the process of forgiveness. Determine that you won't allow bitterness in your life, that you'll deal with your negative feelings until they're resolved, but be patient with yourself as you do so. Look for the freedom that God gives. Pray for it. Search for it. But don't bind yourself with impossible bonds of perfection in the process.

People who have forgiven are much happier than those who haven't. Sheilah came up to us several weeks after a seminar and said, "Thank you for what you shared. I went home and wrote my former husband a letter. I told him I knew I had contributed to the divorce and that I was sorry for my part. I also told him I had forgiven him for his part." The woman beamed, her face radiating the freedom we'd talked about. "You know what?" she said. "He wrote me back a friendly letter!"

Anna also spoke words of forgiveness to her ex-husband. She wasn't sure how he'd receive it, but she found a time to do it. Her ex-husband's response was, "You don't mean it." But her forgiveness had been verbalized, and with this came a great release.

In both cases, the women experienced great freedom. When we forgive, we set ourselves free to be everything God intends us to be. Don't bind yourself with cords of unforgiveness. Let go! And let God show you how wonderful life can be.

This forgiveness of yourself and others—including your ex-mate—puts you into a new mode of living. You are free to grow, to be who you are and most importantly to pursue God's will for your life. You won't need marriage to feel complete.

Moving Ahead

If your journey as a whole person moves you toward remarriage, we want you to be aware of some things to discuss before taking that giant step. So from here on, we switch gears. We'll share some of the things nearly all who remarry face.

How can you cope with those overwhelming feelings of love that often lead to a premature wedding? How can you best prepare for stepparenting? How do you get ready financially? How do you build and keep a beautiful marriage? And what is the best foundation for a solid marriage?

6

We're Madly in Love . . . So We're Getting Married

"We're getting married. What other conclusion is there? It was meant to be!" "I've never met anyone who understands me like she does." "I've never met anyone who makes me feel the way he does. How can it possibly matter that we've only known each other for three days? We're different from the rest."

We wince when we hear people talking this way. Words like these are red flags of warning—to us as counselors, and to a couple who could be heading for a disastrous marriage. There are a lot of red flags, but they're all usually accompanied by one of two possible attitudes. "We're different. It won't happen to us." Or, "I know there are a few little problems, but I'm not worried. Things will change after we're married." But things *don't* change after the wedding. And divorce can happen to *anyone.* What are these red flags? In the next chapters we're going to deal with four of the most common.

Love Conquers All

Romance. It's a big, booming business. And it feels so

good. "Let's always feel this way," you tell each other, but it's impossible. The natural high of being in love is impossible to maintain. You can fall in love with each other over and over, but you can't live in this euphoria. Sooner or later, reality strikes.

This is why God defines love as a decision rather than a feeling. The Bible speaks of *doing* love one to another.[1] Marriage has to be a commitment, because the feeling of love is like a butterfly. It comes and goes.

"But we're desperately in love, and love conquers all!" Few people marry because they hate each other. Most of us *are* "desperately in love," but almost half of our marriages end in divorce. What happens to "love conquers all"?

The truth is that many of us marry for the wrong reasons. And when the first marriage ends, we marry again—still for the wrong reasons. "Thirty-seven Going On Seventeen," is the title of a chapter in Jim Smoke's book, *Growing Through Divorce.* It cleverly illustrates part of the problem. Even in mid-life, we use the same dating standards we had when we were teenagers.

Some friends of ours are great examples of this. They were introduced to each other before noon on Valentine's Day. They began to talk, and continued for 13 hours. By the end of their conversation they had decided to get married. Teenage behavior? Yes, but both these people were in their early fifties. The romance industry thrives on this kind of story. And our culture sets us up for it by promoting an emotional love as the deciding factor in marriage.

When we became Bud and Kathy Pearson, we were old enough to know better. But looking back, we realize we got married mostly because we were "madly in love." We were sure everything would be wonderful. After all, we had been dating for a year and a half and we understood each other so well. We knew life together would be beautiful. It's difficult to admit there was so much we didn't consider, so much common ground we still had to establish. But it's true.

Marriage Will Meet All My Needs

What wrong reasons contribute to the failure of marriages? Perhaps the greatest is the tendency to seek out someone in order to meet our own needs. We've all been hurt. We often feel rejected. So we search for someone to change this, to soothe the hurt and make it go away. As long as we look for exterior solutions, we won't come to understand ourselves—who we are, where we've been or what we want from life.

Tammy came to us with a puzzling question. "Why do I keep marrying the same kind of man?" she asked. She had been married several times, and all her husbands turned out to need a great deal of emotional support. Through counseling, Tammy began to see that she had a very strong mother instinct. She wanted to take care of people, and although intellectually she didn't want to mother the man in her life, it kept happening. She projected a strong image, dependent men were drawn to her, and she kept marrying them.

For many of us, the needs of the moment demand a relationship with another person. We feel lonely, worthless and helpless. And instead of using our time to find out why, we blindly search for someone to take those feelings away. And when we find someone who is interested in us, it's the best feeling in the world.

"God brought us together," you tell each other. "We communicate so well, it's amazing." And all this happens in the artificial atmosphere of dating. You go out together once. Both of you look, feel and act your best. You call each other during the week and go out again the next weekend. Within a short time, you begin to live psychologically as if you're already married.

During this time, when everything is new, both people in the relationship concentrate on meeting the other's needs. The tendency is to be mirrors for each other. He likes bowling, so she develops a sudden interest in bowling. She likes strong men, so he begins to work out at the gym.

While you're busy meeting each other's needs, you're becoming bound to that other person. The reality of who you are and what you want from life gets pushed into the background. Love feels so good, and the emotion so overpowering, that you feel as if you can sacrifice everything else. Your relationship is so beautiful and so fulfilling that before you know it, you're involved sexually. You've surrendered the leadership of your lives to your drives and your needs.

After this, there's only one thing left to do. Get married. And what do you bring with you into the marriage? All the things you didn't deal with while you were busy pursuing a mate. If this is a second marriage, and you haven't dealt with your past, all the junk from the first marriage comes along too.

One year we participated in several marriages, two of which we knew were bound for disaster. We had counseled both couples, urging them to wait, but they were Las Vegas bound if necessary. One of the marriages lasted three days, the other nine.

We don't have ESP, and we didn't put a hex on these marriages, but both couples responded to our cautions by saying, "It's different with us. We're in love." The truth is, that any time a marriage is right, it's worth waiting for. It's worth being absolutely certain both people are ready.

Do you think he will take care of you financially? Do you expect her to keep your house clean? Do you assume he'll release you from making decisions? Do you think you won't need to iron your shirts or remember your mother's birthday? Are you looking for someone to help you discipline the kids? Do you expect her to make your life exciting? These and a hundred other false assumptions doom thousands of marriages almost before they begin.

We counseled Henry, a widower, who said, "I need a mother for my children." Our response was, "Your children will be gone in a few years. Then what will you have in common with the woman you plan to marry?" Often when someone says, "I need a mother (or a father) for my children," what they're really saying is "the burden of being a single parent is too great." And it's true. The emotional, financial, and physical burdens of being a single parent are tremendous, but marrying someone to relieve that stress can make you long for the single life in the end.

God Brought Us Together

"The Lord brought us together," is another remark we often hear. All reasonable evidence to the contrary, you often assume the only thing that counts is your mutual faith. Marriage becomes some sort of mystical destiny—the Lord's will for your life—rather than a personal, rational choice. Christian love is supposed to make all things possible, so you ignore the red flags, believing the Lord will make everything work out.

This attitude can also cover up a basic unwillingness to wait for the Lord's best. Although celibacy is God's gift to some, most single people would like to be married. Almost 97 percent of those we've counseled feel this way. Many of us are afraid God will give us an enforced celibacy without giving us the gift and desire for a single life. Because we're afraid of this, we sometimes don't want to wait for the person of His choice to enter our lives.

You think, "God's standards are so high, I'll never get married." You're afraid of being alone for the rest of your life. But the truth is that if you accept less than God's best for you in marriage, you will have an unhappy life, full of despair and disillusionment. Something will eventually break if you're united with the wrong person. Either the marriage will break up or it will be full of turmoil. Remember, second best is usually second best over nothing. It's almost impossible to live peacefully in a situation that's ultimately against what you want and who you are.

This Is Our Second Marriage, So We Really Understand Love

Another wrong reason for marriage involves our lack of understanding about what love means. Feelings of love are almost like infatuation. They're wonderful, and God gave them to us for us to enjoy. We all love to be in love. It's a natural high. But it doesn't make a marriage.

Life always runs in cycles. You get up some mornings and feel great. This terrific sense of well-being follows you throughout the day. *I've finally got myself together,* you think. *At last, I've got it made.* And you really think it will always be this way.

But a few days later, you get up out of bed, and zap! You didn't want to get up in the first place. It's a crummy day and the world owes you a vacation. You can't stand the person you see in the mirror. You finally get to work—late—and everyone is out to get you. The whole day is rotten!

This is the cycle of life. No amount of vitamins, exercise, or positive thinking will change it. In Southern California, we always have bright, sunny weather. Except when it rains. But when it rains, we know one thing:

Eventually we'll see the sunshine again.

This is God's world. He doesn't intend for you to function on the basis of your feelings. Life requires decisions. And love is a decision, *not* a feeling. There'll be times after you're married when you won't feel as if you're in love. In fact, sometimes you'll feel as if there's less than nothing there. But when you *decide* to love, it will always be a fact of your existence.

Dr. Robert Merkle says, "There's no such thing as falling out of love." True love is a decision. As you experience times when you aren't in touch with the emotion of love—perhaps even feel the opposite of it—you can proceed on the basis of love anyway. You can be certain your feelings of love will return, and you can do the loving thing because you have decided to love that person all the days of your life.

I Know There Are Problems, But They'll Change After We're Married

A third thing that destroys marriages is when one partner becomes involved in trying to change the other. What happens to the things you hide, overlook and excuse while you're dating? Like skeletons in the closet, they come clattering out. Then you begin to work on each other. A little change here, a little change there, and your spouse will be just right. Because you went into the relationship to have your needs met, you continue pushing for your needs to be realized in the other person.

Rarely does a man and woman marry without some idea that they will change each other after they marry. The results of this assumption are devastating because, without realizing it, each person is planning to play God in the other's life. Instead of wanting their mate to become what God wants, they're actually wanting their mate to become *what they want.*

We have developed an iron-clad dogma for those who are contemplating marriage. If you can't accept the person you're in love with just the way he or she is, without any changes or reservations, don't get married. Otherwise, you will begin to manipulate.

Manipulation violates a person's need to be accepted and loved without reservation. The primary mode of manipulation in marriage is nagging, but nagging only makes us cling more strongly to our irritating habits. People don't change for external reasons. Change comes from within, and it comes as we grow and mature. But the process is divinely orchestrated by God, not humanly plotted by our spouses.

This doesn't mean you have to wait for a perfect person. Since no such human being exists, it would be fruitless. It does mean you must take a serious look at the things you don't like and make certain you can live with them. Small things that seem unimportant when compared to the intensity of our feelings, become extremely important later. One couple we know argued about the way the toilet tissue was put on the holder—to roll it in or out. Sometimes, the most insignificant things become important in everyday living.

Check out spiritual values. Is he mainly interested in material things while knowing and serving God is the highest priority of my life? Is she pursuing worldly knowledge while growing as a Christian is what I'm committed to?

Check out attitudes. Does she have her mind made up about things while I'm still searching out the options? Does he save every penny while I like to spend? Does she want to live in the country while I like the city? Is he easy-going while a well-kept home is important to me?

Check out interests. Does she like contemporary music while I only listen to classics? Does he watch football all weekend while I think it's uncivilized?

Check out habits. Does she eat everything in sight while I carefully watch my calories? Does he sleep with the shades up and all the windows open while I need a warm, dark room?

Check out life-style. Does he stay indoors while I like to climb mountains? Is she reserved and thoughtful while I'm outgoing and impulsive? Know your likes and dislikes, be sensitive enough to see others as they really are, and you will know how compatible you'd be in a marriage relationship.

Opposites Attract

"Opposites attract," the old saying goes, but it fails to add one important word—"temporarily." Opposites attract temporarily. At first you're fascinated by your differences. It feels good to be around someone who likes you, and yet projects qualities you don't have. There's a vicarious pleasure in it, and you tell yourself, "Well, two halves make a whole." But the truth is that two halves make two halves, and two wholes make two wholes.

God wants each of you to be a whole person. The more alike you are, the more potential you have for a good future together. In the beginning, you may struggle with competition, but as you seek to build a good marriage, you'll learn to complement instead of compete with each other. And because you're so much alike, the chances for understanding and mutual goals are greatly increased.

Ask yourself, "Are we best friends? Do we confide in each other? Do we trust each other? Do we share a spiritual closeness? Do we have similar interests? Do we have the same attitudes? Are we emotionally stable? Do we have compatible goals?" The list goes on, but the important thing is to ask the *right questions* and wait for the *true answers* before deciding to marry.

There's So Much Pressure, Maybe We Should

Outside pressures are also a wrong reason for marriage. This statement seems self-evident, but its logic becomes clouded in real life. In counseling we often hear, "I knew I shouldn't get married, but . . . . "

Angela was in her fifties. She began dating Ronald, who very quickly brought up marriage. Because of her age, she thought this might be her last proposal. She felt he wasn't the right person, but after enduring his constant arguments for marriage, she gave in. The marriage turned out to be just as bad as she feared it might be.

When you finally give in—for whatever the reason—it's as if you've plunged over Niagara Falls. The process is set in motion and there seems to be no way to stop it. *I know it isn't right, but I can't disappoint everyone. We've had a shower. We've talked to the minister. The photographer's been hired.* Your thoughts run to all the physical details, and the guilt you'd feel at breaking it off seems too much to bear.

Peer pressure can be just as strong as family pressure. If you've dated anyone for some length of time, the pressure from other singles can be tremendous. If you're in your late teens or early twenties, marriage can become the thing to do. Everyone is doing it. If you're older, perhaps divorced or widowed, marriage is still the thing to do. Everyone's doing it. And those who aren't "just don't have a chance."

Sex before marriage is another enormous pressure. The guilt associated with it often causes one or both people to feel, *We'll get married and that'll make what we're doing acceptable.* Attempting to reform the past, they begin a marriage based on guilt and sexual attraction. The guilt festers and grows, while the physical attraction turns into boredom and dissatisfaction as they discover they have nothing in common.

Living Together Is No Good

What about living together? Many people feel it's a good way to "try marriage," before actually committing themselves to the relationship. But it's the worst thing you can do if you want a successful marriage.

Some interesting statements appeared in *Cosmopolitan* magazine in an article called "Living Together Is a Rotten Idea." After interviewing many women, the author concluded that when people marry after living together, their marriage has less chance of surviving than if they'd simply been promiscuous. It went on to say that those with the best chance for a successful marriage are those who wait for sexual fulfillment until after marriage.[2] Our counseling experiences have borne out this conclusion time after time.

Marriage Is the Ultimate

The last wrong reason we want to mention is what we call "the final resting place syndrome." When marriage is seen as the end rather than the beginning, it's almost impossible for it to be a success. Philippians 2:12 says, "Work out your salvation with fear and trembling." This means to actively participate in making your salvation work for you. Our salvation is a one-time event. It's a ceremony. But salvation life is a dynamic, growing, changing reality.

The same principle applies to marriage. Marriage is a one-time event. But married life is a dynamic, growing, changing reality. For success, you must *build* your marriage—giving here, taking there, changing this, fixing that, relaxing now, pushing ahead then.

The best marriages are those in which both people

only have one desire for each other—that they become everything God wants them to be. This attitude allows freedom and encourages growth. And it fosters blessing for the marriage.

The Real Purpose of Marriage

We believe God designed marriage for our benefit. In marriage we can say, "I'm for you and you're for me." In a world of fierce, uncaring competition, marriage is a place where you can demonstrate love, unity, caring, peace and God's desire for His world.

He wants the world to watch and marvel at the love and unity they express. The silhouette of marriage is two people, face to face, saying, "I am for you." With the right preparation for remarriage, this can become a reality in your life.

7

The Kids Are Excited Too

We often took Kathy's children with us while we were dating because we wanted them to feel included in our blossoming relationship. Usually we did something simple like go to the park or the beach. We knew it didn't have to be expensive. They just needed to feel loved.

After Bud proposed, we took the kids out to dinner and announced our engagement. As we showed them Kathy's ring, they laughed and said, "It's about time!" The kids thought it was wonderful. And we were sure we'd be one big happy family.

Our wedding was marvelous—everything we had expected it would be. As we were married outdoors by the Statue of the Good Shepherd at Garden Grove Community Church, the blue skies spoke to us of more than just the weather. Our life together would be perfect. Lauree and Connie, lovely in their bridesmaids' dresses, and Mike, proudly standing next to the best man, radiated their congratulations. Tears even streamed down the girls' faces as we said our vows.

After the reception, we kissed the kids good-bye,

gave them a few added instructions for the eight days they'd be home alone, and waved farewell. Kathy had raised her kids to be perfect children. We'd spent a year and a half getting to know each other and letting the kids know that Bud cared for them. We were certain they'd be waiting for us when we got back—three perfect children (17, 15, and 10) in a perfect house, ready to start our perfect marriage.

On the seventh day of our honeymoon, we decided to go home early. We were having a wonderful time, but felt ready to be home, and we wanted to spend Sunday with the kids before going back to work on Monday morning. As soon as possible, we called the kids to tell them we'd be home in the late afternoon.

It was 7:30 on a Saturday morning, and no one answered the phone. Certain that everything was fine, we had breakfast and called again. Still no answer. "They must be sleeping in," we told each other as we drove down the mountain. Again and again, we stopped to call. But there was no reply.

Finally we reached Riverside—only an hour from home—called, and Lauree answered. "We'll be home in an hour," Kathy told her excitedly. *We're going to be a real family in just a few minutes,* she was thinking, *and there's so much love between us, it'll be wonderful.*

"What?" Lauree asked, sounding a little dazed. "You're not supposed to be home until tomorrow."

"I know, but we've decided to come home a day early," Kathy replied. "Isn't that neat?"

The phone was silent. Lauree couldn't think of anything to say. When Kathy hung up, she told Bud, "They aren't too excited about seeing us. They must have had a great time while we were gone."

Looking back on it now, we can laugh at the comedy that greeted us as we drove up to the house. At the time, though, there was nothing funny about it. The activity in the front yard looked like a home movie on fast forward. Lauree was in the driveway washing Kathy's car as if she were in a car washing race.

Mike was in the front yard mowing the grass as fast as he could run. *This is awful,* Kathy thought, *but I know the inside of the house will be under control.* A quick walk to the front door told us differently.

There in the living room was Connie desperately vacuuming the rug. A peek into the kitchen convinced us the dishes in the sink were a week old. There was no hiding the fact that the house had been a disaster the whole time we were away.

The kids had been living in total freedom. And they were having a fabulous time! We hadn't been able to reach them because they'd been at the beach all day. They hadn't missed us a bit. We had left them a list of things to do, but failed to tell them *when* to get them done. Of course, they'd planned it all for the last minute. We'd given them permission to drive the car, but neglected to tell them not to drive it from sunup to sundown.

While we were off having the week adults dream of, the kids were home having the week teenagers dream of. Now we were together again, ready to begin our happy family, and we were furious with them for spoiling our plans. Our expectations crashed up against reality, and our beautiful new family shattered in the process.

We both exploded. Kathy was angry because she expected her kids to show Bud how wonderful they were. Bud was angry because he felt it was his job to back up Kathy. We had both agreed Bud would take over as the authority in the home, and now he was determined to do it. But this only complicated matters. Now Kathy was angry with Bud for being angry with her children, and Bud was angry with Kathy because she didn't appreciate his efforts.

Within moments, our newlywed high was destroyed, and its loss devastated us. It took a year and a half to resolve all the repercussions of our homecoming. During this time, we came to see we'd set ourselves up for a gut-wrenching fall by failing to understand the complexity of what the children were going through.

We expected them to want our marriage as much as we did. We actually believed they would help us build the beautiful marriage we desired. We expected our new family life to come together as easily as something from an old-fashioned movie. Our expectations of the kids were unrealistic, partly because we didn't understand the effects of divorce and remarriage upon children.

Adapting to a Single Parent Home

In the beginning of their lives, children have the security of a biological family. Even though there may be problems in the marriage, and many of those problems may affect the children, there's tremendous security in knowing that Mommy and Daddy are together.

After a divorce, children must adapt to a single parent home. In this environment they usually receive the full attention of the parent they're living with. Often, they begin to function as a substitute spouse. They listen to problems, discuss household issues, make plans, and help with the work. With their custodial parent, they become a new family unit. And perhaps for the first time, their help is really needed. Mom or Dad depends upon them. The kids are an equal part of the household equation.

As their parent begins to date, kids are plagued by questions. "Will he try to take my real dad's place?" "How can I like her and still love my real mom?" "If they get married, will I still be important?" "Will my parent still need me?" Many parents, unaware of the questions in their children's minds, fail to discuss these things.

The engagement is announced, the wedding date set, and the important things haven't been talked about. Even though the couple has included the children in their dating, they haven't prepared their children for what happens next. In a remarriage, it's just as important to talk about these things with the children as it is to discuss them with your spouse.

Children need to be told the basics—that both of you love and need them, that you want to build a good marriage and a happy home life, that everything won't be perfect but you'll work to solve problems together. They need to know that they can ask questions when they don't know what's going on. They also need to be told practical things—what the dress code will be around the house, how the household responsibilities will be divided, how your home style will change.

Learning to Be a Stepfamily

For the best transition into stepfamily life, you must talk with the children regularly and often. And you must listen, taking their feelings into account. Most of us act as if the kids will pick up our plans by osmosis. The fact is that most children are so busy trying to cope with their jumbled feelings, they can't even think of the questions.

Discovering who the children are must begin even before the marriage. Although you spend time with the kids while you're dating, you are still a guest in their lives. Unless you make a determined effort to learn who they are, you won't really know them and you won't be ready to live with them.

Children can't be ignored after the wedding, and you can't become a real stepparent to them until you first become a trusted friend. Find out what their lives have been like before you came on the scene, what their values and standards of behavior are. Learn what their goals are, who they admire and who their friends are.

Look for the whole picture, observe what has gone on in their lives—not from a critical perspective, but because you truly want to know them. Spend time alone with them. Let them know you're interested. Remember, love is a decision.

Make the decision to love the children, just as you made the decision to love their mother or father. Determine that, by God's grace, you will love them. Search for agape love, drawing on the love of Christ to quicken your commitment to them.

If you love the kids consistently, if you prove through your actions that you're worthy of their trust, you will receive their love in return. Even if it's not there at first, sooner or later they'll love you back. Actions are more important to children than words. Lead, don't push. Show them you love them by giving them a positive role model to follow.

Let the kids know their parent is the most important person in the world to you. The best gift you can give children who have been through divorce is the security of knowing that it won't happen again. As they observe your love for their parent, as they watch a good marriage at work, their attitudes about marriage and family life will change and they'll be given hope for the future.

Kids are afraid the new marriage will end in divorce. Rita said, "My teenage daughter never told me she worried about my new marriage until one morning when my husband and I had a minor disagreement. She came over to me sobbing, "I don't want you to get another divorce."

Children's fears about their new homes extend even so far as to believe that if this marriage breaks up, their parent will leave and they'll be stuck with the stepparent. *After all, Dad left the first time, so if it happens again, Mom will go and I'll be left alone with someone I don't know,* they reason.

Single parents often develop a special closeness and camaraderie with their children, turning to them for security in the aftermath of the divorce. After the remarriage, kids often want to turn back the clock so they won't have to share the limelight with a stranger.

Kids also have a natural desire to see their biological parents back together. This desire—an inner longing for the divorce not to have happened—never changes. Reality is difficult to accept, even for mature adults. Only as the adults in the new marriage stand together, allow the kids to see the goodness of their new relationship, and wait patiently, can the children come to accept the new reality.

The fear that they won't be loved or needed can hide itself for years before it's expressed. Because they may have functioned as a surrogate mate before the remarriage, the adjustment to simply being kids again can be difficult. Jealousy against the new stepparent can be extremely strong until the children realize it's possible to love in more than one way.

Children need to know that God made different ways of loving. They need to know He's given us the ability to love our mates and our children in equally important, but very different, ways. They need to know that the two don't have to compete. This understanding will set them free to be children and to get on with their own lives.

Mike was only 10 years old when we got married. Shortly after the wedding he asked Kathy, "How come he gets to sleep in the same bedroom with you?" Before we were married, Kathy's door had always been open. Now it was closed, and he had to knock when he wanted to go in. Kathy didn't think to discuss this obvious change with Mike before it happened.

The changes in home style can be equally frustrating for the new parent. Something as simple as the change in numbers can be bewildering. But it's imperative to realize that you had a choice and the children didn't. You chose them and their parent They didn't choose you. You're getting what you asked for—whether you realize it or not. They're getting something that was put upon them by circumstances beyond their control.

Changes That Occur for Kids

Think about the changes that have occurred for the kids. Something as simple as a name change can be traumatic. Their mother may have a new name. When they get to school and sign their names on all the forms, a name different from their own will go under parent or guardian.

The house may change. Their room may change. Rules change. Furniture may change. Family traditions change. Siblings may change. Numbers change. City, school, church, and friends may change. Relationships change.

There are numerous books on stress currently available. Many of them give a test which lists stress factors and give each factor a certain number of points. When you reach a given number of points in a year, the books say you're a candidate for a mental and emotional breakdown.

Most of these stress factors happen to children in a divorce and remarriage situation—often in rapid succession—and they reach the breaking point. Kids don't know this intellectually, and they can't explain how they feel. They aren't mature enough to figure it out. On the one hand, they may be excited about their parent's remarriage. On the other hand, their emotions are very negative.

Love, understanding and time will heal the dichotomy they feel. Create an atmosphere that is nurturing, loving, and trusting before you ask too much of them. Never forget, they aren't responsible for the traumatic events in their lives.

Authority in the New Family

When you marry, encourage your new spouse in disciplining the children. Talk about it privately, show a united front, *but always remember the discipline belongs to the biological parent.* Later, when trust is developed, you can be an authority in the children's lives—naturally and easily. If the kids are young, you can discipline and train them as any parent would. If they're teenagers, you can be a trusted friend, a role model they can respect.

No matter what age they are, let them observe you over a period of time. Be a friend, but not a pal. Let them know you're an adult who has their interests at heart. Earn their trust. Let them discover that you've joined their household for better or for worse. They need this security, but it can't happen overnight. If you don't have the grace to be patient and secure within yourself, don't become a stepparent. The process that brings togetherness takes years, not months.

Don't expect the kids to be like you. They aren't. Don't try to mold them after you. It won't work, and you'll feel rejected. Your discipline will backfire, and your self-esteem will suffer. Don't grasp for a role that's impossible. Don't set yourself up for problems you can't solve.

If your stepchildren had a poor home situation in the past, don't expect to be their rescuer. Regardless of what has molded them, it's already happened. Respect it. Respect the children's past and *both* of their biological parents. No matter how wrong things have been in your judgment, the kids must salvage as much respect for their roots as possible in order for them to be healthy. Let God use you for healing, not division. And rmember, divorce is *not* a brief crisis. It takes years for the children to recover.

Because it takes so long to blend styles and to establish ground rules in a new home, let the kids know—by word and deed—that you're around for the duration. Let them know it's OK to love you because you won't be going away. Let them know you care about them as individuals, and not simply as extensions of the parent you married.

Becoming a Stepparent—What Do I Do?

Three remarriages come to mind as we think of stepparenting. In one of them, Karen had complete authority for her children, and Sam wanted it this way. He was never involved in disciplining them. Although this disturbed Karen at first, she accepted it. After they'd been married for two years, something serious happened with the children. Feeling overwhelmed, Karen asked Sam to step in. He did, and the kids responded very well. By this time, they were sure he cared about them. They knew he really loved them.

The second example is more typical. Ralph married Leslie who had small children. Determined to be in charge, he began telling the kids what to do right away. He wanted to form them after himself as quickly as possible. The kids were nervous wrecks. They didn't know how to handle his expectations. They didn't understand why something had been OK before, but now it was a major offense. And they were completely bewildered.

The third example brings us to Paula. She married Joe, who had two children. All she wanted from them was to be their friend. Paula told them, "I expect from you what I'd expect of anyone in my home. I expect you to clean up after yourself, to let me know where you are, and to be courteous and respectful. Simple rules." The kids loved it, but because he had some expectations he had never talked about, Joe found it difficult to accept. He wanted Paula to be a super stepmom and she refused the role. He wanted her to be the mother to his children that his first wife had never been. Wisely, Paula realized she could never fill that role, and it was only through good communication that they came to an understanding.

The truth is that children's biological parents are and always will be their biological parents. Whatever the truth of their heritage, they need to make their own peace with it. If they are young when you marry into their family, you will completely father or mother them in the years to come. But you will never replace their biological mother or father.

Unless there's been a death, your kids have two biological parents somewhere. Even if one of them is dead, the children will still identify with that person. No one can ever take their place. It's wrong to think you're doing the children a big favor by taking over the role of their missing parent. It's asking for trouble to say, "I'm your new daddy." Or "I'm your new mommy." The kids know they already have one of each.

Don't be surprised by the small things if you become a stepparent. We were married only nine months when we took a trip across the country to visit Bud's parents. Everyone was excited about it until it came time to leave. As the kids trouped out to the car, each with a pillow under an arm, Bud shook his head in bewilderment. "You're not going to take those pillows," he said, wondering where they'd fit everything.

"Oh yes, they are," Kathy said. The trip began with tension, and we didn't understand what was going on until later. Kathy had taught her kids to sleep on long drives. Bud thought long trips were for animated discussions, pouring over maps, pointing out and visiting sites of interest. From the beginning, our expectations were different and neither had thought to ask the other, "What do you do on long trips?"

Stepparenting is difficult because of the kids' history without you. You weren't around when they were born. You didn't feed them or change their diapers. You weren't around when they said their first word and took their first step. You didn't watch them grow and change, becoming who they are now.

When you look at the children, you don't see yourself in them. They don't have your values. They don't have your habits. They don't have your likes and dislikes. They don't have your looks. They're completely different from you. And the natural delight of a biological parent, seeing yourself mirrored in your children, is not there to fall back on in times of stress.

Consequently, you feel left out. And rather than wait for this identification to develop naturally over the years, there's a strong pull to make it happen. This is a fatal tendency, and it kills marriages. The number one cause given for divorce among remarried people is "the kids."

We hear it over and over again. "It's the kids' fault." "We couldn't handle the kids." "The kids just couldn't adjust." "The kids rebelled." Our response is, "Who are the adults in the situation? Did you try to manage the kids, or did you try to build your own relationship?"

Let the children be responsible for themselves. Don't assume the situation is hopeless because you can't make them happy right away. Major on each other. Accept the kids where they are. Let them have their feelings. Let them take responsibility for their actions. Love them, and give them time.

It's an unfortunate fact that most children feel responsible for their parents' divorce. Even as early as the age of three, many of them assume it was their fault. They hear their parents fighting—often about them or the complications of family life—and they assume the divorce wouldn't have happened if they didn't exist.

We asked a group of high school students at a seminar, "How many of you feel responsible for your parents' divorce?" Sixty percent of them raised their hands! With so much guilt and turmoil, is it surprising that kids have a difficult time adjusting to a stepparent?

Never allow yourself to forget two important facts. The children aren't responsible for the breakup of their first home. And they aren't responsible for the success of their second. You chose them. They didn't choose you. It will be up to you to make the relationship work.

God's forgiveness is complete and beautiful, but many of the scars of divorce will always remain. The broken relationships include not only husband and wife. The relationships change between the children and both parents—even the one with custody. Many others have been hurt by the divorce as well: parents, grandparents, relatives, and friends. All these relationships change. And when you enter into a remarriage, you must learn to relate to everyone.

Don't try to replace the ex-spouse in the kids' lives. Don't try to influence their feelings for the parent who is outside the home. No matter what the other parent's problems may be, that person is the biological parent of your stepchildren. Accept him or her without judgment. Determine that your presence in your new family will be for peace, not division.

8

We'll Move into Your House

"You have everything we need. Your house is large and beautifully decorated. And conveniently located, too. We'll just move into your house," you tell each other as you make plans. It makes perfect sense. Or does it?

The most controversial advice we give on remarriage is to find a new place to live. "Begin brand new—even if it's in rented housing with 'early goodwill' furnishings—rather than risk the pitfalls of 'mine and yours,'" we tell couples. But it's easy to contemplate this advice and conclude you're an exception to the rule.

At our first seminar a man stood up and told the group, "Listen to what these people are saying. It's only been three weeks since my second divorce. When I remarried, it seemed ideal. My wife had three kids and a beautiful home full of nice furniture. It seemed logical for me to move into her house.

"The first time we had an argument, she said, 'If you don't like it, you can just move out. It's my house.' I knew she didn't mean it because it was said in the heat of anger. I knew she loved me. But the next time we had an argument, the same thing happened.

"I began to feel like a whipped puppy standing in a corner with his tail between his legs. Because I hadn't invested anything in the property, I felt it really was all hers. This created so much antagonism and hostility between us that we finally got a divorce."

It Seems Financially Sensible

The financial expediency of "moving into your house" is difficult to resist. "If we sell our houses and furnishings to start again, it will be expensive," you reason. "We'll lose a lot of money." It's true. It's expensive to begin again—especially in the middle class life-style.

At first, we weren't aware it could be a tragic mistake to "move into your house." When we married, it simply wasn't an option. Neither of us owned a house or lived in an apartment big enough to accommodate five people. Between us, we had little furniture. But since then, we've seen this issue bring more unhappiness into remarriages than any other. We've watched it bring an end to what were potentially good marriages.

How much is your marriage worth? Is it worth the very best chance of survival? Is it worth all you can give to make it work? Is it worth more than money can buy? If your house and your present life-style are more important than your marriage, do yourself a favor. Don't get married.

If you want the best marriage possible, give yourself a clean break with the past. Sell your beautiful furniture. Keep a few special things, but get rid of the rest. Settle your financial matters. Sell or rent your house. Set aside what you wish for your children's inheritance. Then give yourself a starting point after which everything will be "ours." Live in a happy hovel if need be, rather than in a contentious manor.

But take care to do it with a willing attitude, motivated by love not coercion. If you give up your material things reluctantly, you'll bring emotional baggage into the marriage. Before you're aware of it, you'll become historical in your thinking. "It cost me $20,000 to marry you and now look what I'm getting for it," you'll find yourself muttering.

It's difficult to be honest when you're dating. You're madly in love, and it's hard to believe everyday concerns will matter so much. But after the marriage and the move-in, the feelings come as if from nowhere. Not wanting to admit them, not wanting to appear irrational or immature, you'll tend to displace those feelings and argue about unrelated issues or simply give in to depression.

Talk these practical arrangements out before marriage. Again, communication coupled with a willing attitude is the key to success. Allow for the possibility that you may fall into the trap of "yours" and "mine." Commit yourselves to make everything "ours" and plan for it. Tell each other, "Whatever we achieve from now on will be ours."

We counseled with Tim and Carla, a couple who seemed to risk none of the problems of "moving into your house." They had no children, and neither of them were living where they'd lived with a former spouse. His place was conveniently located and she liked it, so they decided to move into it.

After they were married for a month, Carla came to our office and said, "If you ever need someone to stand up in front of a seminar and say, 'Don't move into each other's house,' I'll do it. We get along great. We have no problems—except for his house.

"Every time I move something, Tim says, 'Didn't you like it there?' And when I change something, he says, 'I liked it the way it was.' It's a continuous battle." Fortunately, they handled the conflict with mature attitudes. They solved their problem by renting his place and buying a home of their own.

If your new spouse lived in the house with his or her former mate, the potential for trouble is even greater. Imagine a woman whose husband leaves her. She lives in the house for several years, changing a few things here and there, but basically leaving it the same. Then she marries again, and her second husband moves into the house.

On their first night after the honeymoon, he sleeps in *his* bed. The next morning, he wakes up to shower in *his* bathroom. Then he goes out to eat on *his* table and read the morning paper on *his* chair. Suddenly, the new husband has emotions he never anticipated. His external surroundings remind him of his wife's first marriage rather than pointing him toward their own new beginning.

Imagine further that this woman has children in her custody. But on weekends, her first husband comes to visit the kids in the house that used to belong to him. He plays ball with them in his front yard, gets some of his things out of the garage, and showers in his bathroom before he takes the kids to the zoo for the afternoon. In the meantime, the second husband feels like an intruder.

Yours, Mine, or Ours?

When couples marry for the first time in their late teens or early twenties, everything is *ours*. They bring almost nothing of their own into the marriage, so everything belongs to them—not yours or mine, but ours. The object is the same in a later marriage or a remarriage—everything becomes *ours*. And yet, it's incredibly difficult to make this transition when so much has been *mine* for so long.

We tell couples that it's worth the pain of losing their belongings. Planning for the future, working from common goals and common funds, expressing who you are together in your physical surroundings—these are essential building blocks in your new relationship. Time, energy, and money spent on a new beginning result in a harmony and unity that's priceless.

Your togetherness is more important than anything you own. By starting fresh, you're giving your marriage the potential to achieve common goals. Young marrieds don't expect to start out having everything their parents do. Yet remarrieds, often unrealistically, expect it all.

Jayne had a beautiful big home which was worth a fortune. When she decided to marry, she sold her house so that they could have a home of their own. Harold was a retired military man with a healthy pension, so she told him, "We'll use my money to buy our house and furnish it. We'll use your money for everyday expenses like the car, groceries, and clothing."

Without realizing it, Jayne was encouraging Harold to put his money into consumables while she kept hers in fixed assets. When guests came to visit, she would show them around "my new house" and point out "my new carpet," and "my landscaping" without realizing what this was doing to her new husband.

Eventually, they had an argument about an unrelated issue and Harold put a cot in the garage to sleep on that night. This became a pattern. Every time they had an argument, Harold went out and slept on the cot. After a while, he walled it in and make himself a little room. Then winter came and it was cold, so he went to a motel. In a few months, he simply left, and the marriage was over. This couple might have built a beautiful marriage with good communication before making such unrealistic plans.

It Will Be Best for the Kids

Many couples begin their marriage "in your house," intending to change this down the road. "We can't financially handle a completely new start right now," they tell each other. "But a year from now, we'll sell it all and buy new things." A year has an uncanny way of remaining "a year from now." It never comes.

Other couples have children to consider. "Isn't it better to keep the kids in their own home where they can stay in their own room, have the same friends, and go to the same school?" they ask each other. At first glance, the obvious answer is, "Yes. Let's not put the kids through any extra changes." But on closer examination, this logic is faulty.

If you believe a child's greatest security is to have parents who love each other and are committed to each other for the rest of their lives, the need for unity in the new marriage becomes primary. The kids need your marriage to be stable. They need to be able to count on you. They need a peaceful, loving home.

Also, children can be very possessive about their own environment. They often resent changes in their lives and tend to treat the new stepparent as an intruder. Because it's their turf, it's easier for them to put the stepparent on the defensive. After all, it's their house and their things and their way of going about life.

This can make adjustment difficulties seem like the kid's fault, when actually the fault lies in not having moved to a neutral location. Bob had a pre-teen daughter. They were very close and secure in their father-daughter world. And when he married, bringing his new wife to live in his home, his daughter couldn't accept another woman in the cozy home she'd built with her father.

In another case, Anita and her children moved into

her new husband's home. Jerry had never had kids before and his furniture was scratchless. She was bringing children into a home where everything stayed in its place. Soon Anita was hearing, "Get that kid off my couch." "Don't let him mess with the vase." "Oh no, not dirt on the carpet!" The effect was unintentional, but devastating because she translated this to mean, "I don't want *your* kids in *my* house."

Most of us assume remarriage means leaving all the past behind. But in reality our thought processes keep it alive. Particularly when the end of a first marriage is unwelcomed—as in the death of a spouse—the tendency to compare is overwhelming. If the second marriage lives in the surroundings of the first, it's almost impossible to resist.

The stories of trying to forge a new marriage on the remnants of the first go on and on. Jim and Marge thought they couldn't afford to move, so Marge bought half the house before they married. Although this took care of who owned the house, it didn't take care of his history there without her. After a year, nothing could change the fact that Jim had lived there 14 years while Marge had only been there one.

Frank insisted Terri move into his house. It was the price for marrying him. But he was a man who wouldn't change a thing. Six years later, everything is still exactly the same. Terri has stayed in the marriage because she is totally committed to it, but she is often miserable. Frank has big heavy masculine-looking furniture. Nothing in the home looks like her, but he won't allow her to do anything about it.

Adam, a wealthy businessman, owned a home and let his daughter run it after his divorce. She was redecorating when he decided to remarry. Only during a counseling session did he realize it might be a mistake to bring his new wife into a house his daughter ran and had just decorated.

Donald came back to see us a year and a half after his remarriage. They had moved into Betty's house because she had children. But soon after their marriage, his son came to live with them as well. Betty's children couldn't accept this. The son was an unwelcome guest, and Donald soon heard the heartbreaking words, "There's no place for me here, Dad."

There's good reason to make a new place for yourselves in your new marriage. Make a place that belongs to the two of you. Welcome the joy of creating something that expresses your love and unity. Give each other the best of yourselves, not simply of material possessions. Tell yourselves, "This marriage is completely for us. It will never be mine and yours, but always ours."

9

Everything Will Work Out Financially

. . . And, yes, the bum you were kind to last week is actually a dying billionaire who will leave you all his money because you're the only decent human being he's ever met. Silly. But many of us approach our finances in a vague fashion that doesn't make much more sense than such a fantasy. *Somehow it'll all work out,* we think, often avoiding the uneasiness inside by simply spending more money.

Finances are usually cited as the second major cause of divorce among remarried people. Often, it was a problem in their first marriage, and nothing has changed. Rather than educate themselves about finances while they were single, they simply muddled along hoping things would get better some day.

Use the time before you marry to learn about your money. Learn to manage your money rather than letting it manage you. If you are living under the burden of debts with your spending out of control, understand that it's possible to live differently.

The joy of using your money well, of living within

your means and of living without the burden of debt is well worth the effort it takes to change. This peace of mind and feeling of self-control and self-determination will be an essential boost to your new marriage.

Discuss Finances Before You're Married

If you're planning to be married soon, it's time to talk about how you'll handle your finances. Most couples just assume everything will work out financially. They have a broad idea of how the money will come in and whether they'll be rich, poor, or in between, but they don't discuss money beyond this.

Once again, communication coupled with a willing attitude is the key to success. Discuss every aspect of money you can think of. Ask each other questions. "How do you feel money should be handled?" "How do you feel about borrowing?" "How do you feel about spending?"

Express your feelings. Feel free to disagree. Be willing to compromise. Find an approach to finances that you're both comfortable with and make practical applications. If you don't, you'll pay later with continuous confusion over finances.

Who will manage the money after you marry? And how have you reached this decision? "It's the man's job," isn't a good reason. Sometimes the woman is better at managing money. Sometimes, they both enjoy it and want to divide the job. Who manages the money and how they do it isn't nearly as important as agreeing upon a plan. No matter who actually pays the bills, both of you should know where the money is going and have an equal say in it.

Don't keep secrets about finances in your marriage. This only fosters mistrust. Don't build a nest egg on the side "just in case." This escape clause only weakens the commitment necessary for the health and healing of a marriage. The answer to financial disagreements is to communicate, communicate, communicate.

The best time to start building unity over finances is before your marriage. At this point, financial issues aren't as emotional as after you say, "I do." This may seem obvious, yet most couples we counsel shake their heads and say, "I don't know," when we ask them how they'll handle their finances.

Some situations clearly demand discussion. If there's a great dichotomy between two people in their material wealth, it begs to be discussed before marriage. Very wealthy people will wonder if they are being loved for themselves or for the money, and will wonder how to arrange the finances after marriage so they are equitable. But those of us who have nothing, very little, or an average amount, often don't consider it a topic for discussion.

"It's always worked out before," you tell each other. "We love each other. That's the only thing that matters. The finances will fall into place." Clay and Anne Marie came to us for premarital counseling. He was a certified public accountant and she was a corporate bookkeeper. When we asked them who would handle the finances, they both appeared startled. They'd never talked about it, but of course, Anne Marie thought she would and Clay thought he would.

Some couples don't talk about finances simply because they don't have any money when they marry. Others don't discuss it because they were raised in homes where money was private and it was bad taste to talk about it. Some people have had such difficult experiences with money that they simply aren't open to suggestions.

If your financial situation is complex, you may find it necessary to get professional help in planning for your marriage. Stu and Margaret, a couple in their late fifties, both had sizeable estates. Because they wanted to preserve most of this for their children, they sought financial counsel, putting much of it in trust funds before their marriage. Then they pooled what was left and said, "This is ours. Whatever this builds into is our own estate."

Mark and Rachel, a younger couple, did a similar thing. She had property and he had business investments. They both wanted a contract agreement before their marriage, so they got legal advice. Generally, a third party is only necessary if you can't communicate satisfactorily or if your affairs are so complicated that you might make a mistake you'll regret.

Ed and Peggy failed to do this. They were madly in love. After the marriage, she discovered he was deeply in debt. At his urging, she took the money from the sale of her house and paid his debts. But their financial problems continued because Ed was always in debt. Their marriage ended in divorce, and Peggy was left in financial limbo.

The most important aspect to finances in marriage is unity. Steve and Lois decided to have separate checkbooks since they were both producing income. This wasn't an error in itself, but they did it without an attitude of togetherness. Lois worked and kept her paycheck, paying all her own bills. Steve worked and did the same. Financially, they were operating as if they were single. Neither knew about the other's money and neither felt obligated to help the other if there was need. Each considered their money *mine*, rather than *ours*.

Take your financial temperature before you marry. Can you discuss money and not become angry or defensive? Do you have a desire to share your finances with each other? If your mate is unable to work, will it bother you to be the provider? And when there are children will you be willing to meet their needs?

Our culture has changed a great deal in recent years. Often the man assumes it's the woman's responsibility to work outside the home. Usually, she was working when they married and he takes it for granted that she'll continue. But some women want the time to be homemakers, especially after children come. Discuss your priorities before marriage, so you won't come to grief afterward.

If you're planning to marry someone who already has children, whose responsibility do you think it is to care for them? Harriet already had several children when she married a man whose attitude said, "I've already raised my family and I don't want to raise somebody else's." They didn't discuss it, but Allen put the entire responsibility—financial and otherwise—on her for her children. Needless to say, the marriage was very difficult.

What about retirement? Some people expect never to retire, and others can't wait. What about savings? Some people spend it while they have it, and others save for a rainy day. What about wills? Who will get your money if you die? How do you feel about spending money on clothing? On entertainment? On travel? On education? On kids? On tithing? On household items? On cars? On investments? On insurance?

When we married, we didn't discuss our finances beyond the fact that we both wanted to tithe. We knew we were starting with nothing—less than nothing since we had debts—and we agreed to stay current with these obligations, no matter what. We were madly in love. We believed the Lord wanted us to be married. Beyond this, we didn't talk.

God provided a wonderful rented house for us at several hundred dollars below comparable houses in the neighborhood, and we began our life together with bits of secondhand furniture. We hadn't talked about who would manage the money, how much it would cost to raise and educate three kids, and what our financial goals were beyond paying off our debts. Both of us had managed the money in our previous marriages, and it was a shock to discover we both intended to do so in our new marriage.

Our solution has been to share the managing of our money. We've learned to talk about it regularly, and to find unity when we disagree. Several principles have become clear to us. One is to make it simple. Good financial management doesn't need to be complex.

Get it down on paper. Calculate your income, subtract your fixed expenses, and come up with the money you have to manage. Keep track of all this in a simple ledger. Income on one side, and expenses on the other. Don't worry about locating every dollar, but keep a running record of where the bulk of your money goes. (See diagram 1.)

In our home, we have a family file. The first file folder is the family budget. Inside is a monthly budget for each of us. We have separate checkbooks, but they contain both our names and the money in each account is "ours."

This makes it simple to find out where we stand at any point. We just look in the ledgers.

All this sounds simple, but most people don't cover even the elementary basics of finances. One woman told us, "I'm mad at God." When we asked why, she said, "Because my checkbook is overdrawn." When we asked her if she'd balanced it lately, her answer told us her checkbook wasn't God's fault.

Another principle is that the only money you really manage is the difference between income and fixed expense. Fixed expenses are *fixed,* although we tend to

Monthly Budget

Income

____________	$ ______
____________	______
____________	______
____________	______
Total	$ ______

Income $ ____________
Less
Outgo ____________

BALANCE $ ____________

The balance is the amount of money you have to manage each month. It reflects your financial liquidity.

Outgo

Tithe		$ ______
Savings		______
Mortgage/Rent		______
Utilities		______
Elec	$ ______	
Gas	______	
Phone	______	
Water	______	
Other	______	
Car Payment		______
Car Maintenance		______
Gasoline		______
Food (Markets and Restaurants)		______
Clothing		______
Loan Payments		______
Credit Cards		______
Insurance		______
Auto	$ ______	
Medical	______	
Life	______	
Home	______	
Other	______	
Taxes and Social Security		______
Recreation/ Entertainment		______
Home Maintenance		______
Other		______
____________		______
____________		______
____________		______
____________		______
	Total	$ ______

think of them as sums to juggle. "I make $2,000 a month," someone says, and the impression given is that there's $2,000 to spend. But on closer examination, a lot more than taxes are subtracted from this figure. All fixed expenses—housing, utilities, time payments, insurance—must be subtracted as well. If you make $1,800 a month after taxes and your fixed expenses are $1,500, then you only have $300 to manage each month. This is hard to accept, and the temptation is to lie to ourselves.

Credit Cards and How to Handle Them

At this point, people get themselves into financial trouble. The money is in your hands before you pay the bills. You can buy new clothes or take a vacation. You wrestle with your conscience, and then give in to the temptation to spend it on something that will make you feel good.

Later, a red notice arrives in the mail. Your only solution is to borrow. And the easiest way to borrow is with that credit card you haven't quite used up to its limit—that simple, irresistible plastic money. You use it to pay the bill—or to buy groceries so you can use the grocery money to pay the bill—and you hitch a ride on the credit card roller coaster.

There's a foolproof solution to the credit card dilemma. Have a credit card party! Get out all your credit cards except one. Find a large wastebasket and some scissors. Cut the credit cards in half and drop them into the basket.

Then celebrate your freedom. If you don't have the cards, you can't use them. Make a solemn vow about the major card you've kept for identification and emergencies—that it will only be used if it's absolutely necessary.

It makes perfect sense to get rid of your credit cards and get the peace of mind that comes with being debt-free. At the time of this writing, interest on credit cards is above 20 percent. Think of all the things you could have bought with the interest you're paying. If you have a balance of $2,000, that's more than $400 you could have spent on something you'd like to have if you'd been willing to wait for it.

And there's an interesting dynamic that comes with credit cards. If you have a ceiling of $1,000 on a card, the chances are great you'll keep the balance close to $1,000. You'll pay the minimum monthly payment, maybe pay it down to $900, and then charge it up to $1,000 again, forgetting how much you're paying for the privilege of being in debt.

Soon a letter arrives from the credit card company. It says, "You're such a nice person and such a good credit risk that we've decided to increase your limit to $1,500." This makes you feel wonderful, so you go out and charge the card up to its new limit. This happens on several cards until one day you wake up, total the cards, and realize you owe an enormous amount of money. Now you're paying for the sheer joy of staying awake at night wondering how you'll ever pay off your cards.

The Bible says to owe no man anything. There is a sound spiritual reason for staying out of debt. God wants to own you—body, soul, and spirit. He wants you to belong to Him alone. When you're in debt, you belong to your debts. They own you. You're a slave to them because you can't walk away from them. You aren't free to respond to the Lord's guidance in your life because you must, first of all, meet your financial obligations. Proverbs 22:7 confirms this. "The rich rule over the poor, and the borrower is servant to the lender."

Living Debt-Free

Another principle we're strongly committed to is to live as debt-free as possible. This means knowing where you stand financially, and living within your means. It means a strong resolution not to wager your future, not to spend your life paying for yesterday. Do whatever is necessary to get out of debt, and determine that you'll remain out of debt.

You're a child of the King. The whole world belongs to you. All of it was made for you to enjoy. You don't need a fancy life-style to be happy. Drive past a mansion and think of how much work it takes to maintain that life-style. A friend of ours once said he found out that when he got the material thing he dreamed of, he didn't own it. It owned him.

If you're not convinced, talk to yourself. Imagine that you've bought a new luxury home. It has to be decorated with the latest furnishings, otherwise why have a luxury home? The yard must remain immaculate, the paint perfect, and of course, you can't have an old car pulling up the driveway. Now imagine that you finally have everything perfect and it looks like a model home. If you and your family live in it, how long is it going to stay that way?

Do you really want to spend your life taking care of your material possessions? Why not store your treasures in heaven where they don't depreciate? Live for the Lord, for the present, and for the future. Don't live for the past.

Alimony and Child Support Payments

Another principle is gracious acceptance of alimony and child support payments. If this is your situation, God requires you to give these regularly and with a cheerful heart. If you put Him first, He promises to care for your needs.[1] Alimony and child support payments are needs.

They're fixed expenses. They aren't negotiable.

If you don't talk this over before you're married, these obligations can cause tremendous problems. Both of you must agree that these come as part of the package—that you won't let yourselves dream about what you could do with the money—or it will become a poison between you that could destroy your marriage.

Your attitude in giving child support must be *I'm contributing to the growth and welfare of my children.* If you're tempted to think your former spouse is living high on your money, stop a moment to examine the facts. Calculate how much it costs to raise a child. As we're writing this, it takes $4,800 dollars a year to support one child. Divide that by 12, and compare it to what you're paying. The truth is that not many parents are paying even half the amount it takes to support their children.

There is only one healthy way to pay alimony. Write out the check each month with a Christ-like attitude, asking God to use the money to bless your former spouse. You've been given an order by the courts to pay alimony whether you agree with the decision or not. Instead of chafing against it, give the money as if you're giving it to the Lord. Ask God to make you willing, and to keep you from coveting what isn't yours in reality.

Tithing—Give to Get to Give

The most important principle in managing your money is giving. Give to the Lord off the top of your income rather than from what's left after you've spent it. Give to Him regularly and joyfully. The Bible tells us, "Each man should give what he has decided in his heart to give, not reluctantly or under compulsion, for God loves a cheerful giver." (2 Cor. 9:7). The Greek word for cheerful here is *hilariously.*

When you understand God's economy, it's possible

to give hilariously. It makes no sense in the world's economy, but it makes perfect sense in God's. Luke 6:38 says, "Give, and it will be given to you. A good measure, pressed down, shaken together and running over, will be poured into your lap."

The imagery of this verse is that of going to an open market, ready to fill your sack with grain. The best merchants will allow you to fill your sack, shake it down, and fill it again until it's overflowing.

The hilarity is that it's impossible to outgive God. He just keeps giving it back. He's so interested in providing for His people that when you become a provider, He just gives you more so you can keep on giving.

Giving to God is a statement of faith and well-being. It's saying, "I can take care of others because I know God's going to take care of me." Giving to God is an adventure. It's knowing, *something exciting will happen to me because He's going to provide for me in a way I can't calculate right now.*

Giving to God is also a wise investment. When you give to God, you're investing in something more solid than stocks and bonds. You're buying into a circle of provision that won't be shaken by the rise and fall of the world's economy. Give to get to give to get to give . . . . This circle never ends.

When we married, we had less than $50 a month after fixed expenses. The temptation could have been to think, *God wants us to eat. If we starve to death, we won't be any good to Him.* But both of us were committed to tithing, so we gave to the Lord off the top of our income. Every month, we had to pray for the necessities of life, and every month the Lord delighted us with His provision.

Some people say tithing is an Old Testament concept. This is true, but Jesus told us to honor the commandments, and then do even more.[2] He wants us to have an attitude of bounty, to live as if we can't give enough. He wants us to pray, "God, bless me financially so I can have the joy of giving it back to you." If you adopt God's way of thinking about money, you'll live the most exciting life possible.

10

Our Marriage Will Be the Greatest

"Our marriage is going to be the greatest," you tell each other while you're still wrapped in the glow of "falling in love." The shock comes later. You wake up and realize that a wonderful marriage isn't automatic, that it doesn't follow love feelings like the tail follows the dog. After the wedding, you quickly learn each other's weak areas and faults. This is why love has to be more than a feeling. It has to be a decision.

First Peter 4:8 says, "Above all, love each other deeply, because love covers over a multitude of sins." This type of love learns to accept each other without holding out false expectations of perfection. It's an unconditional love that says, "I love you. That's the way it was, the way it is, and the way it will always be."

There's tremendous security in this type of commitment. It provides an atmosphere of trust and openness between two people. If you aren't sure your spouse will still be around after you've disclosed your innermost self, then you have to keep playing the game of hiding behind a facade.

Living with a lifetime commitment means saying even before marriage, "I will never leave you, no matter what happens." A marriage, beginning without this commitment, is already in trouble. A man at a seminar told us, "I know 50 percent of the trouble with my second marriage was that I was afraid to totally commit myself again. I believe this lack of commitment had a negative effect on my marriage at every level."

"In sickness and in health, in poverty or in wealth, as long as we both shall live." These words were included in the traditional wedding ceremony for good reason. It's this kind of thinking that will carry you through the rocky times that always come.

We believe commitment to marriage goes further than simply agreeing to endure it. It also carries the resolution to build a good marriage, to work at creating something filled with life. "We will marry, we will stay married, and we will have a beautiful marriage."

The three aspects of commitment in marriage can only be expressed in the plural. Just as it takes two people to marry and stay married, it also takes both to have a good marriage. Because of this, it's crucial to know each other's deepest heart before you marry and to know that each of you will give all you can in the years ahead.

"We're going to build a beautiful marriage." When this is a stated commitment between you, you can return to it for comfort in the stormy times. It's knowing the sun will shine again. It's knowing you can both feel like packing your bags, but neither of you will because come what may, you're in this marriage *together* and you're going to make it *beautiful.*

Communication: The Foundation of a Beautiful Marriage

The foundation of a good marriage is communication. If you can't communicate, it's impossible to have a good marriage. From time to time, we meet couples who say, "We've been married 30 years and we've never had a misunderstanding." Our response, if we would say it out loud, would be, "The truth is that you've never had any understanding." We truly believe these people have been simply co-existing for years.

Inherent in communication is miscommunication. When you risk getting to know who someone really is, you also risk finding out who that person really isn't. Learning how to communicate is a trial and error process. No expert can tell you exactly how to do it, because communication between two people is as individual as they are.

Communication goes much deeper than simply knowing your spouse's likes and dislikes. It involves coming to know who that person is and what he or she needs—just as certainly as you know those things about yourself. It even means learning to feel your spouse's feelings, to put yourself in his or her place, to understand why your spouse reacts in certain ways.

Bryan gave Gloria a big beautiful home on a hill with a gorgeous view of the ocean. He gave her money to have it professionally decorated and to stock the closets with designer clothing. In the garage, he put two Mercedes and he hired help to care for it all. Bryan gave his wife everything—except what she really needed.

He was away most of the year, always busy making more money, and he was never there to tell Gloria he loved her. He was never around to show her how much he cared about her. And he never understood that more than all the material things he gave her, she needed the security of his loving presence. Gloria needed to hear and observe in hundreds of different ways, by his words and actions, that Bryan loved her. She needed to know she was the most important person in the world to him.

Ken was married to Pearl who kept a spotless house. She was very creative and seemed to double their money with the bargains she found. She painted and decorated their house by herself yet it looked professionally done. She was a wonderful mother, a cornerstone of the church, deeply committed to community affairs, and held a full-time job at the bank as well. Pearl was beautiful, intelligent, and hard working. But she never gave Ken the thing he needed most.

He needed encouragement. He needed to know that Pearl thought he was a wonderful guy, someone worth being around. She gave her attention to everything except him. Ken needed to know she was in his corner rooting for him in life. His security was in being known, loved, and admired for who he was. With all her marvelous qualities, Pearl failed to understand her husband's deepest need.

If you don't understand that your spouse's deepest need is the gift of yourself, it's possible to spend a life pursuing the American dream, never truly satisfying one another. This is the gift God gives us—the gift of Himself. He communicates with us. He listens and responds.

Someone has said, "When a woman marries, she exchanges the attention of many men for the inattention of one." The same could be said for a man. Often in marriage, we don't take time to ask each other, "How do you feel about it?" Or if we happen to ask the question, we don't truly listen to the response.

Listening to each other's feelings, helping each other express what's inside and accepting each other's feelings without judgment, all lead to emotional stability and solid relationships. Feelings are emotions. They are involuntary and need not be threatening in any way. Helping your mate work through negative feelings is an act of love and kindness. Rejoicing with each other in good feelings is sharing the best of life.

Because of the complexity of remarried life, there is even more need to communicate in a second marriage. In a first marriage, two people must adjust to new friends, relatives and in-laws as well as to each other. But in a remarriage—especially if children are involved—there are extra sets of everything, including former spouses. It takes a great amount of discussion over a long period of time to resolve all the issues raised by these new and complex relationships.

Open channels of communication come as you're aware of the other person. Perhaps you're a natural communicator, and perhaps your spouse is not. Perhaps he or she has been taught that "if you don't have anything good to say, don't say anything at all." When a problem comes, you may want to talk about it immediately, while your spouse simply hopes it will go away.

If you don't know why your spouse responds in this way, you will probably assume it's because of an uncaring attitude. But if you know that person deeply, you'll understand and find a compromise between discussing it now and never discussing it at all. This is why communication must begin before the problems arise.

Who is she? What does he want out of life? What happened in her childhood to make a particular subject so painful? Why does that make him anxious? Why does this make her so happy? If your courtship has been a good one, you may have asked each other these questions before. But asking them once isn't enough.

You've probably heard the story of the woman who, after 25 years of marriage, asked her husband, "Do you love me?"

"I told you I did when I asked you to marry me," he said.

"But do you love me now?" she asked.

"I'll let you know if I change my mind," he replied.

Most of us aren't so blunt, but it's easy to feel *I've said and heard it all.* We forget that the answers change because we're changing people. Never let the time come when you stop asking, "Who are you? What do you feel?" Each of you are growing and gaining insight and perspective on your lives. If you don't share this with each other, you'll change and grow apart rather than together.

One of the most difficult things in a remarriage is all the past history without each other. Most first marriages occur when people are young and their lives are just being formed. In many of them, the couple grew up together or at least in the same community. In a remarriage or in later marriages, you're more likely to have come from different parts of the country and to have been formed by very different experiences. You will have so much to share and introduce into your togetherness.

Trust is the key to good communication. Without the safety of knowing your words won't be used against you, communication becomes guarded and uneasy. Many remarried people are afraid to talk about their past for fear it will be used as ammunition against them in the future.

We should be a haven for each other in our marriage. "I'm for you. I'm on your side. I promise not to work against your good." As you say these things to your spouse and prove with loving care that you mean them, your marriage will become a safe place to share the deepest parts of yourselves.

In this loving atmosphere both partners begin to feel, *I can pursue life. I have somebody who will stand with me. If I fail, I won't be rejected. I'll be encouraged to try again.* Without this security, there are always doubts and questions playing tricks with our minds. *Why did she say that? What was he trying to get me to do? What did he mean by that comment?* Trusting love believes your spouse only has your good in mind.

Kids: They Don't Come First

Children need this model of loving parents who value each other enough to take time to understand each other. As they see how much you love each other, they'll experience a security you can't give them in any other way.

In this world of divorce and division, children take great pride and delight when they can say, "My parents really love each other. They like each other. When they have problems, they work them out. They enjoy being together."

This model gives your children security now. "My parents are going to stay together. Nobody's going to break up our family." And it gives them hope for the future. "If my parents can have a good relationship, then it's possible for me to have a successful marriage when I grow up."

Be good to yourselves. Be kind to yourselves. Your relationship with one another is the most important thing in your lives. It's more important than your parents or your friends—or even your children. Children can't have a happy life unless they have a happy home. And the atmosphere in your home is determined by the atmosphere in your marriage.

One of the best ways to demonstrate the unity in your marriage is through physical affection. We often hear people say, "But we don't want to show affection in front of our children." Oh yes, you do! You need to hug and kiss and hold hands frequently. You need to say, "I love you," when they can hear it. It's essential for your children to see an active love relationship between their parents—even when one of them is a stepparent.

Children think it's fabulous when their parents are communicating and having a good relationship. Kathy's ten-year-old son walked in one time when we were kissing in the kitchen. "Oh, you two lovebirds," he said, "You're so silly." But the pleasure he felt was evident in the grin that covered his face.

Getting Away from It All

Although two people may be open and willing to communicate, the pressures of daily life often prevent this from happening. You jump out of bed, rush through breakfast, put in a full day at work, and fall exhausted before the television at night. If you only communicate when there are hassles to resolve, hassles and communication will begin to mean the same thing to you. And in your natural tendency to avoid problems, you'll also find yourself avoiding communication.

The importance of making communication a pleasurable experience and of giving a positive glow to the mere thought of it can't be overstated. Getting to know each other should be fun. If you find that you've only been talking about the kids and the job and the house, run—don't walk—away for a vacation together. Make a pact that you'll share only the deepest parts of yourselves—your feelings and desires—while you're away.

Getting away can take many forms. You don't even need to go away from home, although it usually helps. The most important thing is that it's fun for both of you. Getting away simply means stepping out of the ordinary routine, saying to each other, "I'm taking time out because you're the most important person in the world to me."

How about a late night swing in the hammock on the

patio? A walk down to the drugstore for an ice cream cone? A drive to the beach to walk in the sand? An unplugged telephone and a closed bedroom door.

Praying together is a wonderful way to "get away" and communicate. Often our deepest selves become more apparent when we're before the Lord even though they've been hidden from us. Seeking counsel together from a third party can also help to shake loose blocked areas of communication.

When we look at the changes in our society since the turn of the century, it's easy to understand why you can be in your spouse's presence and still not be together. If you lived five miles from your nearest neighbor with no telephone, television, or radio—not to mention home computers and video—your life would center around your home and the people in it. But in today's world, hundreds of options take you away from the home you're trying to build.

Even when you're together at home, you can become distracted by other things. The television's on, the newspaper has just been delivered, the telephone is ringing, the kids have the stereo on and a car's pulling up in the driveway. Sometimes it's absolutely necessary to get out of the house in order to give yourselves fully to each other. "But is it good for the children when we leave them with a sitter?" we're frequently asked. Our answer is that what's good for the parents is good for the children.

Focusing on Each Other

We counseled Mike and Trish several years ago, and participated in their wedding. Between them, they had five kids—three of hers, two of his. It was a blended family. About a year later, Mike called on the telephone.

"We're splitting up," he said in tears. As we talked, he

shared that the problem was with the children. They were always fighting and pitting the parents one against the other. "We come home from work and it's just one hassle after another with the kids," he said. "And the weekends are even worse."

We asked Mike when was the last time they went out together to talk—just the two of them—and he said, "Never. We've never done that since we've been married." Mike and Trish had put themselves into a fiery furnace anyway. Blended families are never easy. But without taking time for themselves, their situation was hopeless.

This emphasis upon each other refreshes and replenishes a marriage. Couples often find they're tearing at one another simply because they don't feel valuable to each other. Whatever you're fighting about is really beside the point. A fight means that too much time has gone by since you've heard, "You're important to me."

Without quality time alone together, all your contact with each other becomes performance oriented, and each of you begins to feel used in the relationship. But when you spend time with each other, the message gets through. Many problems will resolve themselves just in the knowledge that your spouse cares.

A psychologist friend, Dr. Frank Freed, always says, "There should never be a time in your marriage when you aren't looking forward to doing something together. And when you do something together, then immediately begin to plan something else."

Sometimes couples object to this idea because of the expense. But creative ideas don't need to cost a lot. Dinner at a fast-food place can be great. Sneaking out for breakfast is wonderful. Window shopping in a mall is terrific. The important thing is that you're together, majoring on each other. Develop a list of "our favorite things."

Burt and Diane took a vacation in Europe. They stayed in a fancy hotel, ate at fancy restaurants, and saw all the sights. When they returned three weeks later, their marriage was no better off than when they left. Why? Because they didn't center on each other. They went to see Europe, not simply to be together.

The commitment, communication, and trust which make a good marriage have the basic principle of acceptance at heart. Mary, a woman with a wonderful and growing marriage, told us, "My husband is not responsible to meet my needs, and I'm not responsible to meet his. My responsibility is to love him and encourage him to be who he is, to be with him and to be his friend.

"In being with a spouse who is also a loving friend, both our needs are often met—especially the need to be loved and needed. But we don't set out to meet each other's needs. We set out to accept who the other is and encourage each other to reach God's highest potential."

Because our Christian teaching centers so strongly on giving of ourselves to others, we often major on the minors and ignore the majors. Wives make their husbands' lunches, but they don't share themselves completely. Husbands fix their wives' cars, but they don't give themselves unreservedly.

It's possible to retire at the end of the day and tell yourself, "I did this and this and this for my spouse." You can feel satisfied with all that doing, but you've been doing "things" instead of sharing who you really are. Perhaps by making things so physically comfortable, you have even fostered a dependency that's preventing your spouse from becoming the independent, mature adult God desires to mold for His use.

If you can't accept your spouse without some changes, you will eventually manipulate. And that manipulation soon colors all aspects of your relationship.

When you try to change another person, the walls immediately begin to go up between you. No matter how subtle your efforts, the message is still the same. "You aren't right for me without some fixing."

Since manipulation is deceitful—it's not spoken or submitted for consideration—the defense mechanisms that build up against it are hidden as well. A whole unspoken code of offense and defense, attack and counterattack, builds up in a marriage.

She doesn't like his clothes so she buys him something "suitable" for his birthday. It's a birthday present so he has to act grateful. But when he takes a shower that night, he leaves his dirty clothes all over the floor and dribbles them into the bedroom. She picks them up. But that night, she has a headache. The next morning . . . .

The scenario could go on and on. Soon both people are reacting to manipulation rather than acting out the love they began with. "Am I being honest?" is an excellent yardstick to measure your actions toward your spouse. If the answer is "no"—for whatever reason—you can be sure manipulation is involved.

Jesus meets your needs by loving you and letting you know that you're acceptable to Him. He gives you the freedom to make your own decisions. And He respects those decisions, even when they're wrong.

Say to you spouse, "I love you, so I'm setting you free to be yourself." Be an encourager, not a discourager. Don't put up barriers for the one you love, open the highways. It's a circle of love that never has to end. You love, so you encourage, so your spouse loves and encourages, so you love . . . .

Ray and Betty exemplify a wonderful marriage. Both of them have had great struggles in their lives, but when they married they were completely supportive of each other. She wanted to take piano lessons, so he did everything possible to buy her a piano.

When they finally saved enough money, Ray thought it was marvelous of her to want to play it—even though she was over fifty years old. Betty played beginning pieces, and he thought she played like a master. She felt the same about him. He was a mechanic, and she was sure he was the best in the world. When she had taken a few piano lessons, he invited 12 or 14 people from the church, including the best musicians, so they could have a night of music at their house.

They hadn't been able to afford a house in good condition, so they had purchased a fixer-upper and were as proud of it as they could be. She had worked along side him, and was terribly impressed with everything he did. She picked out colors and coordinated everything. And when they gave their guests a tour, she would point out all he had done, and he would brag about everything she had done.

Ray and Betty have put the Lord Jesus first in their marriage. They encourage each other to grow in Him. They decided from the beginning that they would be growing, positive people. And because of this, they are. The unity in their marriage is a blessing and encouragement to everyone around them.

It takes two willing people to make this kind of marriage. It's not possible to have it unless both of you are participating. One person can be extremely enthusiastic and have a great attitude so you may get along well, but the marriage will never grow unless both work to make it happen.

This is a major cause for divorce. If one person is growing and the other is not, there's an incredible drain on the marriage. This can't be stressed enough in premarital counseling. There is only one effective tool for motivating an unwilling partner, and that's the direct intervention of God. For someone already in this situation, the only counsel we have is prayer.

In our pre-marital counseling we stress, "If you don't have a growing attitude, marry someone who doesn't either. Whatever your drive for life is, find someone who shares it. If you want a beautiful, growing marriage, wait until you find someone who wants the same thing."

The Big Four in Marriage

We have a prescription for creating a good marriage—four things you can do to build your marriage just the same way you would eat right, take vitamins, and exercise to build a healthy body. Take a pen and jot them down for yourself.

One. Have a date every week. Get out of the house at least once a week and spend part of the day together—just the two of you. No friends, no children, no great agenda. Go out to dinner and talk. Walk on the beach and hold hands. Be together and take the time to fall in love again.

Two. Take frequent mini-vacations. Get away overnight every five or six weeks. Make it a two day, one night affair—longer if you can. Get away from home and its distractions. Concentrate on each other, on revitalizing every aspect of your relationship.

Three. Attend a marriage seminar or conference every year. This is a commitment to an open heart, a willingness to learn. Each time, you'll experience marriage from a somewhat different slant, and learn things to make it better. You'll also meet other couples who are working on their marriages. Active participation in a group with this common goal can be a terrific inspiration.

Four. Read good books on marriage. Be reading them as the week goes by. This is a daily investment in your marriage, a daily reminder that you don't want to be lazy with the most important person in your life. Talk to each other about what you've read. Apply what you're learning to your lives. Talk about the results.

Sex: It's Not Just a Physical Act

God has given two people a marvelous avenue of communication and renewal in marriage. It's called sex. And Christians can have the most fulfilling sex in the world, because the God who lives within them created sex for the renewal of the marriage relationship, for the culmination of intimacy and unity. Is it any wonder that new life results from this experience?

Secular philosophy calls sex a recreational activity, something just to bring pleasure to the senses. But God tells us it's a confession of unity, of two people becoming one. If you follow the lives of those who treat sex as recreation, you'll find problem after problem. God's marvelous gift is being used in the wrong way for the wrong purpose.

God is the author of sex. Many people go to great lengths to educate themselves about it. But unless they listen to the One who made it, they'll never learn its true meaning.

In the sex act, a husband and wife bring every part of themselves into one intense unity. God meant it to be this way. He meant for them to lose themselves in their love for each other. Two whole people coming together—spiritually, intellectually, emotionally, and physically.

During the sex act, it's impossible to think of anything else. Why is it so all consuming? Because God made it this way. He wanted marriage to have a regular time when everything else was forgotten, when nothing else mattered but each other. He wanted marriage to have an oasis of love that no one else could share.

Psychiatrists recommend vacations. The change of

pace renews and revitalizes. The sex act in marriage is like a mini vacation—a place of total love, total acceptance, and total renewal. God is involved in it. He made it. He's there when it happens.

We tell couples to learn everything they can about sex. We counsel them to talk while they're having sex, to communicate what they're thinking and feeling. We even suggest they pray together during sex, thanking God for His gift and the wonderful way He made them.

It's amazing how many couples go through life having sex for years and never talking about it. They assume a sexual relationship just means physical consummation. If this were true, we would be no different from animals. God meant sex to be a total meeting place of two partners in the enterprise of marriage. He knew they would go out in the world and experience fragmentation. He meant for them to come home to each other's arms, to the safety and security of their love.

If you want to experience God's ideal for sex, beware of how you've been programmed by the world. Sort out your concepts of sex and measure them against God's intention. How many of them are misconceptions?

Leave behind the glamor ideal which is based on juvenile hormones. You have a responsibility as a Christian to look further. Shake off inhibitions from your childhood—the ones that say sex is dirty, shameful, and that nice folks don't talk about it. Turn away from the images that television, magazines, and movies have blazed on your mind—the ones that say sex is only good if the bodies are perfect.

Today's philosophy of sex has completely missed the mark. Permissive attitudes actually hide an inability to enjoy sex. Eighty percent of the singles in America are involved in sexual relationships. Because they ignore the way God created them—first spiritual, then intellectualemotional, and lastly physical—the sex they experience is one dimensional.

In addition, they are cheating themselves of the intimate relationship they hope to find. One dimensional sex begins to take priority over everything else. They begin to be ruled by their hormones, spending their energies looking for times and places to have sex. The rest of themselves—the most important parts—are not cultivated or shared.

God says sex before marriage is wrong.[1] If you violate His restriction on premarital sex, you will be hurt. There is no way to prevent this emotional and spiritual damage. It's built into the fabric of who you are. God made sex for marriage. And He made you to need the safety net of marriage to sustain the intensity of the experience.

He didn't do this to deny you pleasure. He did it to protect you and to give you the very best. In marriage, sex doesn't lose its luster. It becomes more interesting and fulfilling as life goes on. Spiritual, mental, emotional, and physical stability—this is God's ideal. This is His gift to you in marriage. Sex is for pleasure and renewal, for unity and the creation of new life.

Communicate, communicate, communicate. If you communicate in love—trusting, accepting, and encouraging each other—you'll create something so beautiful, your marriage will be a blessing to you and everyone around you. And it will express God's intention for marriage—a beautiful unity.

11

We'll Build Our Marriage on the Rock

A large candelabra stands at the front of the church. In it are two lighted candles and a third between them with its wick still virgin. As a symbol of unity, the bride and groom each take a lighted candle and touch their individual flames to the center one. Then they bring the candles to their lips, extinguishing their flames, and only one burning candle remains. As a hush falls over the sanctuary at the elegance of the unity candle ceremony, the minister says, "And the two shall become one."

We watched this ceremony for many years, touched by its beauty, but were vaguely troubled. Then we realized what was missing. "At the end of the ceremony there should be three candles burning," we told each other. "Although the couple has become one in marriage, they remain two individual people. They're not melting into each other. But now in addition to their individuality, they share a common flame."

Since then we tell couples, "Keep your own candles burning." The middle candle represents not only the two of you becoming one, but also the Lord Jesus Christ at the center of your marriage. Now He is the flame that's burning brightly between you.

"It's to His flame both of you must come in your marriage—to be filled with His Holy Spirit and His gladness of heart. Then this gladness will characterize your marriage, making it beautiful to see. The rock upon which you must build your marriage is Jesus Christ."

Submitting to One Another

God did not intend for us to serve marriage, He meant for marriage to serve us. The words in Ephesians 5 are central to our understanding—or misunderstanding—of God's plan for marriage. A great deal of misunderstanding has accumulated concerning this passage.

Much of this misunderstanding stems from where many people begin their reading to learn God's instructions on marriage. Verse 22 says, "Wives, submit yourselves to your husbands as to the Lord." Countless sermons begin with this verse—browbeating the women about submitting to their husbands and allowing the men to believe they're lords in their homes.

We misinterpret Scripture in this way because of our sin. God made Adam and Eve to live together in harmony, but after they sinned, the blaming began. A split occurred between man and woman during the fall. God has been working ever since to mend it, often without much help from His people.

It is disastrous for us to attempt unity between a man and woman by commanding the wife to submit to her husband, without explaining what biblical submission means. Ephesians 5:21 says, "Submit to one another out of reverence for Christ." Implied in this statement is, "Men submit to your wives."

Men are often threatened by the possibility that their

wives can do something better than they can or have an idea that's better than theirs. No one has told them that God wants them to be submissive to their wives. But when husbands begin to submit to their wives, a marvelous thing happens. The marriage blossoms, and the two of them grow closer together.

This passage on marital relationships begins even earlier when it says in verse 17, "Therefore do not be foolish, but understand what the Lord's will is. Do not get drunk on wine, which leads to debauchery. Instead, be filled with the Spirit." God wants us to have true joy, true exhilaration—not the false kind that comes from stimulants. Verse 19 continues, "Speak to one another with psalms, hymns and spiritual songs. Sing and make music in your heart to the Lord, always giving thanks to God the Father for everything, in the name of our Lord Jesus Christ."

We attach super spiritual connotations to these verses, but they're just saying that when you're filled with the Holy Spirit, you'll express gladness to each other. You'll be joyful and happy with each other because you're making music to God inside your hearts, always thanking Him for everything. When you're filled with the Holy Spirit and living in gratitude, you'll have a good attitude. And you'll express this joy to everyone, including your spouse and your children or your stepchildren.

It is in this context of spirit-motivated gladness that God talks about marriage. He says, "Now that you have a beautiful attitude . . . . " He's not trying to pass off a submitted relationship on anyone who isn't a Christian. Now that you have a beautiful attitude, it's possible to submit to one another out of reverence for Christ.

Why is this possible? Because you aren't threatened by each other. You know who you are in Christ. You know where you're going. You know what you're doing here on earth. You don't feel threatened that your spouse might surpass you. You aren't in a spirit of competition. You're glad at heart, restful and at ease.

It's easy to submit now. The walls of defense are down. Phillips translates Ephesians 5:22 as "You wives must learn to adapt yourselves to your husbands." Adapt. When these words were written, the husband was always the breadwinner. He determined how much money they would have to live on, and where they needed to live so he could find work.

God is saying, "Wives adapt yourselves to who your husbands are, what their gifts and capabilities are. Support and encourage them. Make room in your lives for who they are." This is gentleness—power under control. It's not the helpless position of a victim.

In verse 25, God speaks directly to husbands. He says, "Husbands, love your wives, just as Christ loved the church and gave himself up for her." Because Christ loves us, we don't find it difficult to submit to Him. He never forces Himself on us because His love is sacrificial. And when we submit to Him, we get this love in return.

It's easy to understand submission when you understand love. A wife only has difficulty adapting to her husband when he doesn't love her, when his actions toward her aren't loving or sacrificial. When a man acts out his love for his wife and she knows it's a steady love—a love she can trust—she adapts herself to him, knowing the circle of love they share will never ignore or harm her.

Kathy expresses it this way, "I look at my Bud and I know his heart. I know he would never hurt me intentionally. It took a long time for me to learn, but there's a great freedom now that I know this about him. I don't get my feelings hurt so easily, or get upset so quickly, because I can look at his heart and know he truly loves me."

The Ingredients for a Happy, Godly Marriage

This circle of love, of mutual submission and encouragement, begins in a personal relationship with Jesus Christ. Are you allowing God to fill you with His Spirit? Do you have His gladness of heart? Do you have His unspeakable joy deep inside? Are you a person who's living with an attitude of gratitude?

These are the ingredients for a happy, godly marriage. Show us two people who have these qualities individually, and we'll show you a wonderful marriage. No segment of society has more potential for having fulfilling marriages than Christians. Jesus Christ's role in a Christian marriage makes it possible to overcome all obstacles.

As you put Christ first—individually and together—He becomes the focus of your marriage, the one you both are desiring to please. Because Christ is your highest priority, He becomes a mutual goal. Through His active, living presence, He becomes a marvelous mediator. There's a tremendous security in knowing it's "both of us for Him."

The psalmist says, "Delight yourself in the Lord and he will give you the desires of your heart" (Ps. 37:4). And in Matthew 6:33 we read, "Seek first his kingdom and his righteousness, and all these things will be given to you as well." Take these words literally. Believe them with all your heart. Delight in the Lord. Work for His Kingdom. And if you marry someone with this same goal, God will add a beautiful marriage to your life.

You might expect a pastor and his wife to have a daily devotional time with each other—especially when they minister together as we do—but we don't make it a rule for us. We believe living the Christian life means having Christ at the forefront all day. In everything we do—whether it's mopping floors or teaching Scripture—we want God to be present. We want everything to be a ministry to Him. We believe that all day, every day, should be a devotional to Him.

With Jesus at the center—your first allegiance—you can move through the ups and downs of married life with positive attitudes. Most of all, you know your marriage is unto Him, to glorify Him. Since glorifying God rather than meeting your own needs is the desire of your hearts you can learn from everything that comes your way, turning all the negatives into avenues for growth and blessing.

Life is a down trip to some people. To others, it's an up trip. Tell yourself your life will be a journey up. At 21, a friend of ours was in a diving accident. Gary was an outdoor person. He loved sports and nature. After his accident, he was left with minimal movement in his arms and was confined to a wheelchair.

At first he fought what had happened, crying out to God that it was unfair. Then he remembered God's unending love for him, and settled it, knowing God was still on his side. It's a joy to visit this young man. His zest for life is contagious.

He treats his electric wheelchair like a truck, zooming around to the music coming from his fabulous stereo system. His whole day—from feeding wild birds on the patio to sharing the Lord with visitors—is full of meaning. People love to be around him. He just makes them feel good all over. Gary's mother has an overcoming attitude. He was raised to find the best in every situation.

Often our role models hinder us from embracing life. Whether we're aware of it or not, we have been programmed early in life. As adults, the things of childhood continue to represent security to us.

First Corinthians 13:11 says, "When I was a child, I talked like a child, I thought like a child, I reasoned like a child. When I became a man, I put childish ways behind me." God wants you to grow up. He wants you to put away the fears of childhood. In order to grow, you must expose yourself to things outside your comfort zone. Instead of clinging to the known, afraid to venture out into the unknown, you must allow the Lord to be your security.

Gaining a Growing Attitude

How can you take control of your life to have growing attitudes? Submit yourself to Jesus. Realize that no one else is responsible for your happiness, your success, your salvation, your well-being, your fulfillment or your attitudes. You control all those things with the help of the Holy Spirit who lives within you.

It's wrong to expect any of these things to come from another person. Not only is it turning from God as the source of your satisfaction, it also fails the test of love. None of us can withstand the stress of being responsible for another person's happiness. The tension and anxiety this produces is a heavy weight which will drag us under.

Wayne had been married several times. Something had always been lacking in his relationships. "I'm unhappy," he said. "My wife didn't pay any attention to me." But gladness of heart doesn't come from externals, it comes from within. It's possible to be a happy person even if you don't have a good marriage. Most bad attitudes come from guilt feelings over things we've done or left undone, and which distance us from God.

Jesus Christ is love. He is joy. He is peace. He is gentleness and goodness and patience. He is faithfulness and humility and self-control. Jesus Christ is all these things. And He lives within you. You don't have to cast wildly about for any of these things. You have only to acknowledge your need of Him, and ask Him to make these attitudes real in your life. When all this is yours as a Christian, why settle for less?

Take time to smell the flowers along the way. Determine that by God's grace you'll enjoy life. Philippians 4 gives us a perfect picture of God's best. It tells us to think on the things that are honest, just, pure, lovely, decent, virtuous, and full of praise. If you look for God in every situation, a good mental attitude will follow. He is the author of positive thinking and joyful living.

Truly happy people are in touch with God. God has accepted you, so you can accept yourself. God feels good about you, so you can feel good about yourself. God gives you honor and promotion in life because He loves you, not because you jealously guard your own territory.

God wants to give you a gentle spirit. Then you won't need to control others or need to be right. You won't engage in the power struggles which can become an overwhelming problem between a husband and wife. "You're not going to take anything away from me." "I'm not going to give in to you." This sort of rivalry can destroy a marriage. It's a favorite tool of the devil to keep both partners emotional infants.

Determine now that you'll never engage in a power struggle discussion. Instead, come to each other with gentle hearts, take time to understand each other's feelings, be willing for the Lord to change your hearts, and then wait for Him to bring you into agreement. "Submit to one another out of reverence for Christ."[1] Be willing to let Jesus Christ lead your marriage.

A submitted man says, "I don't have to do anything to prove to my wife that I'm a man. Why? Because she knows it. I don't have to act as if going to a marriage seminar is sissy stuff. I don't have to pretend that books are for women and children. I want my wife to benefit from a man who knows how to be tender and loving, who desires to grow in his understanding of a relationship. I don't want anything to do with being macho."

A submitted woman says, "I'm not afraid to speak out if I feel something deeply. I'm not afraid to disagree if I need to. My husband encourages me to be who I am. He has a positive view of me and I find that I share it. I don't have to prove anything to him. He loves me and accepts me the way I am."

Are You Ready for Marriage?

How do you know if you're ready for marriage? A very good test is to study your potential partner objectively. If you can see that he or she is not perfect, and still say, "I love and respect this person," you are ready for a mature relationship.

Marriage is a lifelong adventure. If you don't expect marriage to meet your needs, but rather to benefit both you and your partner, then you're ready to consider being married.

Marriage is a lifelong process. It is lived out in the arena of the weeks, months and years of your future. If you don't expect it to bring you instant bliss, but understand that you're entering a growing-together-for-the-rest-of-our-lives relationship, then you're ready to take a look at marriage.

Marriage is a lifelong communication event. If you've thoroughly discussed love, housing, kids, sex, finances, relationships and most importantly, your spiritual lives, then you're ready to seriously pursue being married.

Finally, if you are at a point in your life that you could live happily as a single adult for the rest of your life, then you're ready to prepare for marriage. Single or married, we are loved by God. His desire is that we seek Him and His Kingdom first.

Resource Books on Marriage and Remarriage

Duty, Guy. *Divorce and Remarriage.* Minneapolis: Bethany House Publications, 1967.

Ellisen, Stanley A. *Divorce and Remarriage in the Church.* Grand Rapids: Zondervan Publishing House, 1977.

Gurnsey, Dennis. *Thoroughly Married.* New York: Jove Publications, nd.

Juroe, David J., and Juroe, Bonnie B. *Successful Stepparenting.* Old Tappan, NJ: Fleming H. Revell Co., 1983.

Miles, Herbert J. *Sexual Happiness in Marriage.* Grand Rapids: Zondervan Publishing House, 1982.

Richards, Larry. *Remarriage.* Waco, TX: Word Publishing, 1981.

Roosevelt, Ruth. *Living in Step.* New York: McGraw-Hill Book Co., 1977.

Shedd, Charlie W. *Letters to Karen.* Nashville: Abingdon Press, 1977.

———. *Letters to Philip.* Old Tappan, NJ: Fleming H. Revell Co., nd.

Wheat, Ed, and Wheat, Gaye. *Intended for Pleasure.* Old Tappan, NJ: Fleming H. Revell Co., 1981.

Notes

Chapter 2
1. See Psalm 103:12.

Chapter 3
1. See Genesis 1:31.
2. See Acts 2:38.
3. See Ephesians 2:12-13.
4. See Matthew 22:36-39.

Chapter 4
1. See Colossians 1:14.
2. See 1 Samuel 9–19.
3. John 8:32.

Chapter 5
1. See John 1:9.
2. See Matthew 12:31.
3. John 4:14.
4. Mark 12:30.
5. See Matthew 7:1.

Chapter 6
1. See 1 John 4:7.
2. Judith Krantz, "Living Together Is a Rotten Idea" *Cosmopolitan*, (October, 1976), p. 218.

Chapter 9
1. See Matthew 6:33.
2. See Mark 12:30.

Chapter 10
1. See 1 Thessalonians 4:3.

Chapter 11
1. Ephesians 5:21.

For information regarding the seminar upon which this book is based, please contact the authors in care of the publisher. Address inquiries to:

Publicist
Regal Books
2300 Knoll Drive
Ventura, CA 93003